WHO ASKED THAT QUESTION?

A non-techy looks at the 21st century

B A R B A R A   H E E T E R

iUniverse LLC
Bloomington

WHO ASKED THAT QUESTION?
A NON-TECHY LOOKS AT THE 21ST CENTURY

iUniverse books may be ordered through booksellers or by contacting:

iUniverse
1663 Liberty Drive
Bloomington, IN 47403
www.iuniverse.com
1-800-Authors (1-800-288-4677)

Because of the dynamic nature of the Internet, any web addresses or links contained in this book may have changed since publication and may no longer be valid. The views expressed in this work are solely those of the author and do not necessarily reflect the views of the publisher, and the publisher hereby disclaims any responsibility for them.

Any people depicted in stock imagery provided by Thinkstock are models, and such images are being used for illustrative purposes only. Certain stock imagery © Thinkstock.

ISBN: 978-1-4917-1445-4 (sc)
ISBN: 978-1-4917-1446-1 (hc)
ISBN: 978-1-4917-1447-8 (e)

Printed in the United States of America.

iUniverse rev. date: 12/18/2013

To my children, David and Susan,
whose thoughtful questions have
pushed me beyond the old answers.

CONTENTS

PREFACE

I have observed the human condition through the eyes of both teacher and counselor in American, public schools for thirty years. Through the heartaches and joys of the students, their parents, and fellow teachers, I was privileged to a human panorama at the close of the twentieth century. Often the stories that unraveled before me were sad and frightening and from my temporary vantage point had scary conclusions. But even then, a distinct human quality seized my attention. Although I continually sensed its presence, the trait *personal power* took time to identify. I finally recognized that all humans possess this quality, though its strength varies even within the same person. A complex virtue, personal power ebbs and flows through us all as it dictates what we have the ability to do—or not. Power is often used in a negative sense as control over others, but I use it here in a positive way: power over ourselves.

Enabling us when it is strong, personal power blends the qualities of self-esteem, self-worth and self-confidence. It clarifies our relationship with ourselves. As often happens when we fuse ideas, the final product is stronger than any one of its elements; it isn't only in geometry that the whole becomes greater than the sum of its parts! And whether we attach the prefix *self* or the adjective *personal* to the word *power*, the quality directs our energy, our actions, thus guiding our behavior. Family therapist Virginia Satir in her book Peoplemaking dubs this quality "pot". In a simple sentence, she writes "sometimes our pot is high and sometime it is low." Writing more recently than Dr Satir, popular television star and psychologist Dr Phil often uses the phrase *authentic self* to describe someone with a strong sense of personal power. The thirty-two years between the two therapists underlines the significance of this aptitude.

Once I was able to pin down the quality, I marveled at its obvious nature in both the annals of my life and my clients. One true story that clearly defines this power, by its *absence*, is that of a single father struggling to deal with his sixteen year old son. When I knew the man, he wanted his son to stop smoking cigarettes, a relatively small problem in today's adolescent world. I suspected that the father's insistence stemmed from his own past addiction, but I had little information for my speculation. After several failed transactions between father and son over the issue, the father began smoking in order to incite guilt in his son. He told me that he felt it important "to reveal first-hand the hazards of the habit" to his offspring. When we drifted out of each other's lives, both father and son were heavy smokers. As often happens when parents feel helpless with their children, this father grasped guilt as a tool. In the period I knew them, the father had little, if any, of what I label personal power in the essays that follow. He was his son's role model, whether he accepted this fact or not.

In schools I came to see how vulnerable we all are without the power affirmed by our own choices and actions. And unless we credit *ourselves* with the changes in our lives, personal power diminishes. The powerful people I meet, as well as *me* on days when my "pot" is high, are mindful of the positive experiences of their lives, never assigning them to coincidence, chance or material goods but rather to their own choices. The center of their control is *themselves*, and they proudly claim ownership.

Cultural trends in this Postmodern Age drain this quality of personal power in frightening ways.

Technology tempts us to assign results elsewhere. Believing that the new kitchen gadget will turn us into better cooks denies our own power. It becomes the G.P.S. on the dashboard that gets us to our destination rather than our ability to read a road map. The choice of font on the word processor deserves the teacher's praise, rather than our perfected cursive. The next generation at the tiller, those who must empower themselves, is becoming more helpless in defending themselves against this depletion brought on by our technical gadgets. It isn't my intention to rehash the high profile, media events involving young people, such things as drugs, suicides and school shootings attributed to the availability of guns, rock music and video games. These are but symptoms. The *roots* of these publicized nightmares lie in the gradual loss of personal power in the young.

American adolescents maintain a facade which disguises the fact that they are frightened in the world of the 21st century. (I have confined my writing to this country, as this was my research lab.) Kids recognize that the powers of technology, combined with materialism, are not their own, not a force from *within* themselves. One gauge of their fear is the lack of questions among them. Their questions, the lifeblood of a culture, testify to the extent of their involvement in life. Questions imply, among many things, a curiosity, and as history shows us, curiosity also propels the species along its evolutionary path. "Why isn't the richest country in the world fighting poverty and racism?" asked Robert Kennedy over forty years ago. We could now add global warming to his question. Instead of a healthy curiosity about their world, many young people at the beginning of the millennium are lethargic and angry because they are intimidated by the gods that dominate the scene.

The worst of this dilemma is a knowledge that the anger and fears of new generations will eventually subside, if the present trends remain. In due time, people will accept their powerlessness, as Huxley predicted seventy years ago in his classic book Brave New World. Except for the questioning pagan of the novel, the characters of Huxley's utopia gain power only through outside sources, maintaining empty lives only bearable through constant use of a drug called *soma*, implying a focus on physical pleasures.

The following essays are not meant to place all American youth or adults under the same umbrella. I recognize that there are exceptions to my statement above, "young people are lethargic." I refer to the majority, as I see it. Nor do I claim scientific proof for my speculations, simply thirty-five years experience with people of all ages— accompanied by an introspective spirit. Striving to give concrete examples, I have written of my own experiences and those of people I have known. I have also tried to keep the essays humorous, otherwise the subject matter would be too heavy, both for readers and writer.

I trust that our mindfulness as adults to the trends of the present age will again provoke questions. Participants question; spectators and consumers do not. If convinced that our power originates elsewhere, we will eventually attribute our joys to the same external source—rather than our internal feelings. With such a shift, we will lose the human attributes of mastery, creativity, self-discipline, and responsibility. Modernity has made life physically convenient, but the spiritual cost is too great.

Barbara Heeter, MEd.

Even to question, truly is an answer.

Shelly Jackson Denham

The search for an answer [the question] enters into the creation of that answer.

Joseph Chilton Pearce

The world we have created is a process of our thinking and cannot be changed without changing our thinking

Albert Einstein

A SHORT LIST OF QUERIES
FOR THE MILLENNIUM

1. WHY, WITH SO MANY TIMESAVING DEVICES DO WE LEAD SUCH HARRIED LIVES?

2. WHY, WHEN WE EAT LESS FAT AND SUSTAIN MORE HEALTH CLUBS THAN EVER BEFORE IS 60% OF THE POPULATION IN AMERICA OVERWEIGHT AND OF THESE, 30% ARE OBESE?

3. WHY, WITH THE MOST ADVANCED EDUCATIONAL AUDIO-VISUAL AIDES AND THE MOST EDUCATED TEACHERS IN HISTORY ARE STUDENTS DISPLAYING DISINTEREST AND EXTREME VIOLENCE WITH THEIR CLASSMATES?

4. WHY, WITH MEDICAL SCIENCE AT AN OPTIMUM HAS THE USE OF PRESCRIPTION DRUGS RISEN ASTRONOMICALLY?

5. WHY, WITH THE GREATEST ABUNDANCE OF MATERIAL GOODS IN HISTORY IS THE YOUNGER GENERATION CHOOSING IN RECORD NUMBERS TO LEAVE US THROUGH SUICIDE AND DRUGS?

6. WHY, WITH A MYRIAD OF COMPUTER PROGRAMS, BOOKS, AND CONSULTANTS ON FINANCIAL PLANNING IS PERSONAL DEBT AT AN ALL TIME HIGH?

7. WHY, WHEN WE CAN CONNECT WITH ANYONE, ANYWHERE ON THE PLANET IN SECONDS IS PERSONAL ALIENATION REMARKABLY HIGH?

8. WHY, WITH EVERY IMAGINABLE KITCHEN GADGET ON THE MARKET IS THE FAST FOOD INDUSTRY GROWING AT RECORD SPEED?

9. WHY, WITH MILLIONS OF BOOKS IN PRINT ARE READING LEVELS OF THE GENERAL POPULATION FALLING?

10. WHY, WITH OUR PERSONAL GENETIC CODE NOW IN HAND ARE DISEASES OF THE IMMUNE SYSTEM ON THE RISE?

11. WHY, WITH A MYRIAD OF DEVELOPMENTAL SPECIALISTS AMONG US ARE YOUNG CHILDREN DISPLAYING LESS AND LESS EMPATHY FOR OTHERS?

12. WHY, WHEN THE YOUNG HAVE ACCESS ELECTRONICALLY TO SO MANY BOOKS ARE THEY NOT READING FOR PLEASURE?

PART I

LOSS OF POWER

THE DEEP ROOT OF FAILURE IN OUR LIVES IS TO THINK 'OH HOW USELESS AND POWERLESS I AM.'

THE DALAI LAMA

WHO ASKED THAT QUESTION?

I never ask questions about sports. Not because I know all the answers. None of the questions dawn on me. But when someone kicks a soccer query my way, I know that the answer is stored. Somewhere. In my school years, I lacked such poise and struggled to find the right ones for those tests thrust at me by teachers. When my textbook failed to supply an answer, I rushed to the encyclopedias tucked away on the resource shelves of the school library. Accompanied by five-year updates in the last book of the series, these sets proved current, at least for the times. Fantasizing then that my parents would surprise me with such a collection, I looked forward to someday harboring all those answers at home. Now I have them all at home. Though not in encyclopedias. Lurking in corners easy to uncover on those ever-shrinking computer chips, answers abound today.

In fact, I can carry answers *on me* with an I-pad. Black and white, answers resolve matters, putting heated debates to rest. In compressed form, storage and revision of answers are no longer a worry. With the mere touch of the Search button, Wikepedia flashes *detailed* answers to nearly everything. And being declared *right* boosts my ever-needy ego.

But where are the questions stored?

Though I doubt it was an original one, I once stowed a question. I kept it to myself. Likely, my question had circulated in the halls of the public high school of seven hundred where I worked; teens gossip as much as adults. But I don't know if this question had ever been asked—directly. Knowing Fay through her high school years, those times when peers and sexuality reign supreme, I wanted to ask where all her teeth were. But feared a fumble. Without a tooth in her head, how did she relate to those appearance-conscious peers? I wanted to ask but lacked that good lead question. Trained as a counselor to allow kids to direct a helpful path, I waited. But in her times with me, Fay ignored her lack of teeth. So I pretended not to notice. Simply put, I shied from sticking my neck out. I knew that her parents had two other children and were poor, working folks in rural New England and such a question felt rude.

I wonder now if Fay was bullied for her appearance in those high school years. I never heard about it through the peer grapevine who often confided in me. And Fay never complained— about anything. Nor did she ever smile. School bullying was an issue in those early eighties but had yet to make it onto the national scene. At the time, gay sentiment in high schools was minimal too. Closets remained tightly closed, at least in northern New England. The word *harassment* was seldom used and remained undercover— hidden in the less official term of "bullying." Now at the beginning of the 21st century, there's the horror of cyber-bullying done in the privacy of homes but visible to the world and legally difficult to control. But my story precedes all this.

Never a behavior problem, Fay made average grades and managed to get through the shame of blatant toothlessness through those charged years of high school. I might have opened an honest discussion with her with a bit of courage and a delicate question. But in the end, she solved the matter without help from the national news—or me. A super salesman recruiter for the Army posed my question to her. And then quickly provided the answer. Fay enlisted and received a beautiful set of teeth from the U S Government. Outside the school atmosphere, Fay might have felt less stress in her dilemma. So I tell myself.

Had I gotten through the stress of that first question to her, the second and third ones would likely have been easier. Questions are mysterious things—behind one forever floats another. The old worry over weather, "Will it rain?" is shadowed by "Did I close the windows, and where did I put that umbrella?" Trailing the worn "How are you?" are many others like "why haven't I heard from you?" But these queries about weather and greetings are tattered by time. The creative ones have never been asked so can't be goggled. Creative questions *dawn* like the morning sun. When the passion is there.

Albert Einstein with a passionate interest in how the world worked had such a daybreak. In Germany in 1894, he quit school at age fifteen. Eleven years later, he managed to earn a doctorate from the University of Zurich. At thirty, still a fledgling in science, he found himself in disagreement with his fellow physicists who had collectively decided that the speed of light varied. These Newtonian physicists were stuck with a false premise, and Einstein strayed from the thinking of his day and suggested a new perspective. "Why *can't* the speed of light be proven to vary? Because it does *not*?" Simple to us now, Einstein's questions took him down a different path than his peers. His fellow physicists had dismissed the chance that light was a constant. Such thoughts were *out of the question* for them—and stopped the creative process that finally lead to the Theory of Relativity. Considered the scientific discovery of the century, Einstein's theory was founded on his dissent.

And it's this dissent that would charm young kids today. Neither Einstein's scientific wisdom nor his IQ (a number with only adult appeal) would impress them. Nudged along by their egocentric natures, kids abound with questions, and those under seven adore stories that dispute facts. It's the unconventional side of life that fascinates them. Before formal schooling, kids *imagine* and identify with heroes devoid of adult logic. With a whole world to sketch in during those training pants years, they have a daunting task, and new possibilities make the job more exciting. But when the generation leaps into puberty, the questions come to a screeching stop. Teens play it cool through that rough patch of puberty—while hormones rage. They may not *know* all the answers but assume that in the 21st century an Internet search will uncover them. Many likely conclude that with so many answers at their fingertips, original questions are exhausted. Their input may feel useless so they look elsewhere—their passions wander.

In this age of technology, there's much to occupy those teens, who often complain of boredom, a passionless state. Social networks in America: Facebook and Twitter: hundreds of television channels, ipods, i-pads, videos, CDs, MB 3 Players, Game Boys, the Internet:

relationships with friends through cell phone and texting. On and on. Some teens are passionate about piercing their bodies and decorating them with ink. Some *do* drugs. And *doing*, rather than *taking* drugs hints of a pastime. Teens are longing to *do* something. Human intelligence peaks between the ages of 17 and 24 so they're likely longing for that feeling of passion.

Einstein needed passion for his daunting ordeal as he faced that community of seasoned physicists. Had he concluded that the older physicists were the *experts*, the Theory of Relativity would not have been his, awaiting instead for a more zealous rebel. And Fay too was passionate in her pursuit; she knew exactly what she needed from that recruiter.

Passion, too often aligned solely with sex, is much bigger than a sex drive that ends quickly with orgasm. Passion is an overpowering feeling at the other end of boredom. Though passion also creates stress, stress is a force that brings on change. If for no other reason than to rid ourselves of it. Scientists now claim that on our evolutionary journey, stress caused by the *lack* of oxygen brought about original life on the planet. Otters may not have developed their webbed feet if one of their ancestors hadn't felt some sort of tension and varied the usual routine—and gone paddling instead. The dolphin and horseshoe crab have remained unchanged for millions of year. Their evolution appears to have ended. This may signal evolutionary success—or a lack of stress in the lives of these hearty old-timers.

Passion brings on stress but finally leads to creative questions: to creativity.

But it's official: creativity has been on the decline in America since 1990—as shown on the Torrance Creativity Test. Creativity does not show up on ordinary, standard tests. But beginning with his question in 1947, Dr Paul Torrance developed a test for this elusive aptitude and administered it to four hundred third graders in Minnesota in the mid-fifties. To validate results, a team tracked the participants for the next fifty years. Were the life works of those who had scored high on the Torrance test at age eight creative? With a resounding *yes* that crushes coincidence, the results have made these tests the gold standard for creativity.

Human creativity needs rescue. That growing endangered and extinct list isn't limited to animals. Creative questions come mostly from those under forty who, like Einstein, have yet to buy into current data about the planet. Joseph Chilton Pearce, who has studied child bearing and rearing in America for the last fifty years, writes, "To live a creative life, we must lose our fear of being wrong." Whether we're right or wrong, creative questions matter. Sometimes validity arrives in the future, but even those questions that lead no where have passion behind them. *Was he a passionate man?* the five word eulogy used in Ancient Greece says it all in five words. In the end nothing else matters.

POWER OUTAGE

I'm intrigued by the story of Chrysler's PT Cruiser. Even for me ordinarily oblivious to car models, the Cruiser is difficult to ignore. Though this car appeared at the close of the twentieth century, it resembles the *mob car* of the thirties. This seemed to me like a sentimental return to the times of yore for a car maker, but Chrysler's Cruiser wasn't a passing fancy. It came about through a sample of humans who had their brain waves monitored. Projective tests revealed fears of chance acts— random shootings. Events such as Columbine, Waco and Okalahoma City were heavy on participants' minds. A mob car would make drivers feel safe—so designers hoped. And sales of the Cruiser proved good. But after its debut came U. S. embassy bombings in Africa: 911: Anthrax mailings: D C serial snipers and outright war with Islamic extremists. The Hummer soon appeared on roadways with an *I can flatten you* message. The Hummer renders the image of an armored tank. Are we back to who carries the biggest stick? Biggest club?

My first car, a jalopy, signaled a lack of cash. So like most young drivers, I settled for speed to show my clout. Sporty car models such as the Ferrari and Porsche broadcast money. Homes like cars serve as symbols and render messages. Manors in the country, along the water or on mountain tops, proclaim wealth. The SUV (Service Utility Vehicle), large and with high horsepower, declares strength and proclaims the popularity of the prosperous nineties. Until high gas prices and America's huge carbon footprint changed the SUV's message—to a self-centered, gas guzzler. As sometimes happens, the SUV lost its mojo.

More quietly than cars and homes, scholastic degrees send power messages through their acronyms. Degrees are publicized by smugly trailing the names of recipients: BS: MA: BFA: MSW: DDS. On and on. Such titles broadcast book learning— and hopefully knowledge. At graduation, the National Honor Society supplies its members with gold neckpieces: visible symbols, similar to cars and homes that announce the graduates with a high grade point average.

I was once puzzled to see the valedictorian take his place at the podium without the Honor Society's gold circling his neck. A perfect four-point average over four years of high school delivers the title so valedictorians forever sport the gold. I thought Rick looked a bit drab as he took his place at the podium without that symbolic scarf encircling his neck. I credited his dull appearance to a family situation and then realized what was missing—that gold scarf. The other honor graduates needed the gold for distinction but Rick had the podium, his private soapbox for the next twenty minutes. Memories of him in the classroom came back to me, and I remembered he needed no badge of gold for recognition.

Like Rick, Dana had no interest in material badges. Any symbol would have been useless to her anyway. Dana a sophomore in the same high school was severely crippled by Cerebral Palsy. She could walk, but it was painful even to watch. Physically handicapped since birth, she struggled to maneuver the crowded halls during the four minute class change. No doubt observing her peers chatting about last night's date. High school boys, self-conscious of their own changing physique shied from even looking in Dana's direction. Nature failed to compensate her with either high intelligence or great beauty. Even as a counselor, I wondered how she kept going. But once I got beyond the horror of her days, I discovered Dana's secret. She didn't define herself by her problems. The only complaint she ever made to me was that no distinction was made at home between her and her three healthy sisters.

Neither Rick nor Dana ever spoke of what they *had*. What did they *have*, really? Rick had parents who didn't parent, and Dana's had next to no control over her body. To my wonder, these two forever spoke of who they *were*. Rick would say "I'm smart," And Dana often said, "I'm stubborn." I saw a invisible kind of power at work with these two. They had power over themselves.

Power is a tricky concept that means different things, depending on who's doing the talking. And who's doing the listening. Like all words, power is an abstraction. Well, all words are abstractions but some represent tangible things: as the words dog or shoe. But *power* is intangible. Money, cars, houses and degrees are only visible symbols of power. Similar to that cute, curly cupid that appears in red with the bow and arrow in mid-February each year, standing in for that intangible feeling of love.

This curiosity I harbor for power began when I saw the word "power" turning up all over 21st century America. In children's TV programs and toys, those places where today's kids begin to piece together their world, names exist like: Power Puff Girls, Power Rangers, Rocket Power. Heroes are *graded* by the amount of power in their lives. Some are weak and not of much help while others abound with the quality. It seems that a hero's power can't be deduced from their actions in these programs; it must be visibly underlined somehow, duly noted on trading cards. But Superman, Batman and Wonder Woman of the fifties, though carrying glitzy names, needed only their actions. In fact, their associates didn't even recognize them when they donned their uniforms—and became superhuman. In the realm of food today, there are Power Bars and PowerAde. In exercise, we now power walk. Then there are power plays, power markets, and power points in certain locations across the globe. In politics, there's "soft" and "hard" power, referring to a number—something a person has rather than *is*.

A lack of physical power plagues those with Chronic Fatigue Syndrome. They're forever exhausted. An official malady for twenty years, long enough to acquire an acronym, CFS plagues millions in America today who lack energy for even the simplest of life tasks. Such fatigue eventually becomes emotional. Victims are emotionally worn-out, depressed. In America, billions are spent on medication to fight such powerlessness. Prescribed drugs are given to 10% of the children diagnosed with Attention Deficit Disorder (ADD) — those kids who are declared powerless to control their attention. A quarter of a million kids who are declared hyperactive and ADD are labeled ADHD and on Medicaid. Not all medication is prescribed. Large quantities of over-the-counter drugs that boast high energy are sold. And rising alcohol use in America suggests feelings of vulnerability. Of weakness.

Such feelings of powerlessness aren't nestled in the heads of millions without cause. The planet is dangerously warming. (An explosive statement when admitted by politicians; fearing the loss of the vote, they avoid the issue of global warming like the plague.) As stewards of the earth, our performance around a warming planet is dubious at best. Extinct and endangered species are increasing as biodiversity decreases. The planet can't sustain the human population growth.

When the power giant Enron collapsed in 2001 it made national news. Enron had been the largest marketer of natural gas and electricity in the United States and had begun to trade in chemicals and coal when they folded. In 2010, the power giant BP had oil gushing for months in the Gulf of Mexico (Much of the media used the verb *gush* instead of spill, which diverted the story away from human error.) And America, *the most powerful country in the world* has a problem today with that tool known as the gun. Troubled young men are committing random, mass murders with automatic, assault rifles, and even the mentally troubled don't seem to have trouble getting their hands on such weapons. A gun can be a tangible power in the hands of the powerless. But such scary news still only carries half the story.

We humans rely on our sense of sight with an *I'll believe it when I see it* attitude, but some things can't be seen. Both Rick and Dana had reason to hide behind symbols but with healthy relationships— with themselves—they stayed in charge of their actions. Controlling actions is a very tough job for teenagers, who are overwhelmed with the need to identify with peers. But neither Rick nor Dana had an interest in controlling others—nor did either ask for a handicap in this game of life. These two heroes of mine both seized the tiller and happily took the consequent credit for their success.

Power isn't visible in front of our eyes in any of the tangible symbols. It's an inside job, in our minds —*behind* our eyes. A bit more famous than my two friends, the Indian leader Mahatma Gandhi models real power. With only his austere lifestyle to present to the world, Gandhi fought passively for Indian freedom on two continents. His *manner* was his weapon of choice in fighting battles. In his years of peaceful resistance, he opposed the existing tax on salt and led his followers to the sea to *find their own salt*. Likely seeing that the earth's continuation depended on his personal power, Gandhi acted— on a very strong incentive.

A SELLER'S MARKET

I've suspected for awhile that I could purchase *anything*. But all doubt was erased when I learned of Gaydars. Clipped to key chains, these devices detect gay men and woman. Prices range from fifty to five thousand dollars depending on the gadget's range. Spelled with a small "g", gaydar refers to the psychic ability to detect a homosexual—no gadget required for the intuitive people among us. The Gaydar product is designed to relieve anxiety eliminating those awkward pauses in budding relationships. As such curious tools emerge, my mother's words wing back to me. In the forties, she used her first ballpoint pen and exclaimed "What will they think of next?" Little did she know that the Age of Acquisition had barely begun.

Long before my time, buying evolved from bartering. Two parties, each with their own survival needs, swapped items after a bit of bargaining. I weed your garden and in exchange you give me some vegetables. What could be more congenial? I'm sorry I missed such precious parleying. But eventually, money appeared and complicated matters. One person in the trading system recognized the chance for profit and became the merchant. Thus bartering evolved to selling. In the twenty-first century, in-line sales complement *on*line ones. And online shopping appears the most popular use of the diverse Internet. Entire television channels are now devoted to sales. Though this last method still requires the use of a phone, it's at the buyer's convenience. Old-time catalogs, more colorful than in the past, endure— as stores can't hold the diversity of items needed today. And those telemarketing agents have offers *too good to pass up.* Such proposals are so abundant in America that there's an official *Don't Call* list as well as efforts to reduce the sales through electronic mail. Unsolicited offers are so frequent, this junk mail has its own acronym: SPAM.

In the sixties, I sold goods in a department store during my in-between summers—those summers when I was a college student, not yet having made that quantum leap into adult life. Department stores as they were known then have now disappeared, replaced by *super*stores. The department store as known from the thirties through the sixties carried *everything under one roof* as did the old country store—though the word "everything" in those days had a smaller definition. I had little money to spend so the employee discount tempted me as I wandered from floor to floor examining the wares on my breaks. Getting no commission, I searched for markdowns, enthralled by the possibilities in what was to me a giant store. As a summer extra, I was tossed from department to department, from floor to floor: selling jewelry, women's clothing, sports, books. On and on. Until, I finally came to rest in lingerie.

Over my head from the start, I knew nothing firsthand about women's lingerie. Lingerie then included foundation garments: girdles, garter belts and bras. I was nineteen, weighed 110 pounds and was five feet four inches tall. And never wore nylon stockings. The foundation garments, I soon learned, held women's bodies together. Girdles were elasticized and went from the waist to slightly below the top of a woman's thigh. Most of the women who bought them were overweight and needed to *lose* weight—not keep it in place. But in the end, customers needed little advice from me. Foundation garments sold themselves. There were fewer choices then, and women knew what they were looking for in this department. And did little browsing.

Today there are underwear departments in stores but generally only sleepwear and underpants are sold—innocent items. The era of the sixties eliminated both girdles and garter belts. Though such times failed at their goal of bralessness. The one-stop shopping of the past has now given way to specialty shops. Specialty stores sell variations of one item: hearts, Disney, socks, scrapbooks, soaps, Christmas decor, candles, flags, teddy bears. On and on. Some superstores specialize in home repair, office supplies— and toys and infants my favorite: *Baby's First Year.*

An entire store devoted to an infant's first year? Though buying has changed in the last century, infants haven't. Except for a crib and high chair, basic stuff that can easily be bought secondhand, the physical needs of babies in that first year are unremarkable— nondescript, genderless clothing: diapers and bottles. And mothers can eliminate the need for bottles by nursing their infants. This shrinks the necessities to diapers and clothing. Infants outgrow clothes in weeks — and in 2013 a vast variety of diapers can be purchased at the local grocery—so what's inside a store devoted to the baby's first year? With two working parents, convenience wins out, and I concede that times have changed. Harried parents are lured by baby things that shorten their task. Teethers can now be bought sewn into baby blankets.

On the other end of infancy lies college so the mid-summer *Back to School* shopping now includes college dorm decoration. The cost of decorating a dorm room today parallels the rising college tuition.

Those color schemes, shelves, refrigerators, microwaves, television sets and storage bins protract parents' role—briefly postponing that dreaded *empty nest.*

The diversity of goods today brings to light previously unknown needs. Cell phones and laptops now established necessities, have color-coordinated covers—that can be matched to specific outfits. And tiring of applauding, when attending tiresome events, spectators can now buy clappers. Clappers do the job while freeing one hand. Also, two hands are no longer needed to squeeze the toothpaste tube; one hand once held the tube while the other squeezed. Now the task can be done with a gadget that holds the tube while a key is twisted. Then there's the pen that holds a computer chip and downloads material, written previously in longhand, onto the computer. The convenient I-Pad now does what the phone and computer did separately— but is easier to transport.

Unlike those bartering times, I can browse today without *any* needs. Shopping has become a leisure activity—entertainment. Enticing shoppers with unusual malls, each boasting flourishes the previous one lacked, merchants know that boredom hinders sales. Only an enchanted audience hangs around. Wearing six pair of earrings instead of one charms buyers with the possibility of multiple combinations. Piercing the skin attracts youth who puncture their bodies in a variety of locations, including places that are rather private—making the exact number of rings on any one body unknown. And different jewelry can always be added. Collecting a *series* of items in the same genre is a popular sport among shoppers. The Retired Beanie Babies, once considered toys, now entice adult collectors.

Shopping on popular cruise lines is a favorite pastime these days. Ocean cruises offer vacations with a variety of activities: games, swimming, snorkeling, movies, plays, and gourmet delights of both food and drink. But the dominant earth activity of shopping remains a favorite on these sailing ships—though the cruise itself is billed to take guests *out of this world*. Cruising travelers have proven themselves serious shoppers, not content with a simple souvenir shop and postcards. Souvenir shops still abound even in classy amusement parks such as Disney, where they're strategically placed at the end of every ride. Stirring hopes that the joy of the venture can be purchased and carted home—in miniature form, as a memento.

Can exciting moments of life be *wrapped*? Can feelings be wrapped? Do purchases really fill emotional needs?

In this quest for variety and excitement, merchants have expanded their range— to feelings. *Security* blankets can now be bought. Between the ages of one and three, kids often become attached to a favorite blanket or toy and cling to it in those stressful moments of growing up. Now the security is marketed *with* the blanket. "Soft clocks" are billed to relieve the early morning's stress of rising. Throwing or pounding these new alarm clocks doesn't affect their real function—according to the makers, they continue to tick. "Power beads" for *faith, justice, and success*" have found their way onto store shelves. And special sneakers, made of stretchy mesh, can be quickly converted to small balls in case the walker becomes bored or anxious and needs to relieve stress. Teddy bears *with feelings* are now available in stores. Customers fill the bears with batting and then *inject* "love, affection, friendship" through a special wheel—before purchase. The bears' implanted feelings are all positive, unlike that poor, puppet Pinocchio who got into trouble with his negative feelings.

When material items fill emotional needs, feelings become disposable.

The origin of the feeling disappears, as happened with the holiday of Christmas. The basis for the holiday in America has long faded. Christmas is the celebration of the birth of the most *non*-materialistic life on record. But buying material items to celebrate the holiday has become so intense that it begins in the fall of each year, sneaking in behind Halloween and before Thanksgiving. Thanksgiving manages to briefly poke its head in— only to warn of the approaching Big Day. Between gifts, decoration, and pre-holiday celebrations, Christmas remains unmatched for sales—when merchants rely on about 40% of their annual profits.

Sales records for all times, in any book category, has been broken by the Harry Potter series that swept across the world just as the 20th century closed. Originally designed as books for children, the series captivated both young and old. Willing to pay any price for an advance copy of the next book, readers seemed hungry for the books' messages. Such sales suggest that the plot touched a cultural nerve. In the story, a school exists where students go to learn magic— acts outside the present rules of life. Kids must discover the right train track as the school's location is tricky. And the train's boarding plank can't be found by just anyone. Only those who have a sincere interest in magic can board the train. (So a GPS, unable to make such a distinction, would be of no help.) With no reference to any technology, the Harry Potter series implies that both feelings and power originate *within* us. But such clout can't be activated by reading or even owning the books.

CHANGE OF HEART

Since I was a kid, things have changed at lightning speed. Though such a statement might be uttered by anyone in any age, comparing the fifties to the millennium is as the English say, like cheese and chalk. In a mere fifty years, we've added e-mail, answering machines, computers, home videos, microwaves, remote controls, calculators, CD's, DVD's, the Internet, fast food, birth control and abortion pills, digital clocks and cameras, cell phones, Velcro, permanent press, Barbie dolls, and paper diapers. Eliminating: tonsillectomies, suntans, typewriters, 45 rpm records, cloth diapers, girdles, mending, penmanship, blue laws, slide rules, castor oil, seamed stockings, cigarette holders, baby walkers, garter belts, permanent wave machines, shorthand, paper dolls and slide rules. Such changes cover a mere two generations. Having lived for a time on both lists, I've had a wild ride.

In the late fifties, I carried a slide rule to math class. No longer in existence, the slide rule was replaced by the calculator and is alien to kids today. Compared to the I-phone, even the portable version of the slide rule was bulky. *Portable* is as close to a description as I can get as *laptop* wasn't an official word then. Hard to imagine now, but the slide rule was a manual tool—neither electric nor battery run, it had only a human charge. Slide rules entailed more math skills than calculators— and with some mastery could perform exotic operations such as square root and logarithms. Large models of the tool were used for classroom demonstration and adorned advanced math classes of the times. Six feet in length and hanging solemnly above the blackboard in the front of the classroom, those demo models proved a commanding sight for me. Not easily forgotten.

At one foot in length, awkward to carry and expensive for the times, my slide rule stayed at my side. I learned that it shared much with the abacus of ancient times. Both tools required skill so learning to use that slide rule taught me a lot of math. Though I was far from fast in my calculations. Even at their best the slide rule and abacus would be far too slow for today's use. Calculators work at a speed in harmony with the computer. But speed was less important then. I cherished my badge of mathematical savvy that I carried to class.

At the time I needed backup for confidence. I was in that transitional state, not yet ready for a quantum leap to full independence, labeling myself an adult. America too was changing. Still sighing in relief of World War II's end a decade before, the country was in the midst of a *baby boom,* as the soldiers returned to start new families—or enlarge the ones that they'd left behind to possibly grow up without fathers. At the country's helm as President was one of the war's grand heroes, Dwight David Eisenhower. Reassuring in a fatherly way, he passed the torch to the youngest man every elected to the high office, John Fitzgerald Kennedy—to start a new era that included the exploration of space. Math and science exploded in school curricula across the country. And the speedy calculator appeared. Stunned, I watch my beloved slide rule fade into oblivion. To antiquehood.

The antique state exists for things like horse drawn sleds, carolers, village stores, gas streetlights, candled Christmas trees and burning leaves. Things that deliver memories and wrap us in romantic lure. Warm fuzzy reminders of a quiet past find their way into drawings and often adorn greeting cards. But the slide rule and things like vinyl records, typewriters and permanent wave machines are too hard— metallic and odorless for the wistful jobs. Maybe tastes will change in the future, rendering even those cold objects fit for flights of fancy into the past. But not yet.

The slide rule's fall into antiquity proved quicker than the calculator's acceptance in public schools; it had a bit of a rocky start as mastery was still a priority in those days. In the sixties, kids were barred from using calculators on tests— especially the standardized ones. Teachers reasoned that *basic skills* would be lost with the constant use of the new tool. Kids would be helpless when the awesome calculator proved unavailable, teachers concluded. But when the pocket version became cheap and their absence looked unlikely, even math textbooks began to encourage daily use of the unique calculator. And soon the English teachers followed by abandoning their emphasis on student penmanship. Word processors could now be used, supplying kids with a legion of fonts— available before they entered kindergarten.

Examining the other changes of the last fifty years, replacements are clear. Barbie dolls are akin to paper dolls of the past. And both Barbie and her clothes are more durable. Vinyl records once provided music, but the newer CD offers a better sound and lasts— well, until they too are replaced. That awkward garter belt of yesterday has been swapped for panty hose. And answering machines, recording devices of all kinds, have replaced the subject of shorthand in high schools, rendering time for other endeavors. Tonsillectomies, suntans, girdles, castor oil, seamed stockings, cigarette holders, and baby walkers have been found either useless or unsafe—and have duly disappeared.

Some changes can be labeled fads and may swing back like the crewcut and Hoola Hoop. Changes dictated by fashion alternate with the season. Styles such as the length of women's skirts and hair rise and fall on a regular basis. Others in the losses column have been outdated, replaced by smaller, speeder tools and are unlikely to return. Using language of the digital age, most *deletions* of the last half century seem firm.

Modern devices of instant communication aren't substitutes for any objects of the past so belong on the progress list. I can now connect with anyone in any part of the world— and leave them a phone message, e-mail, text, *or* fax. The messages are received within moments of them leaving my fingers, and such connections cancel all excuses for neglected friends. Then there's Facebook and Twitter: the social networks designed to keep us in touch. Such innovations generally quiet my qualms about modernity.

Paper diapers are disposable, making them easier for busy parents. The old cloth ones, which in addition to the task of washing and storing often held remnants of detergent, and caused diaper rash. The lack of a rash and the convenience of the paper ones trump criticism. Leaving me with only a few lingering questions. Dumps, worldwide, will be crowded for decades with disposable diapers. (as well as plastic water bottles) But there's a more troubling worry. A recent rise in male sterility throws doubt on the heat created by the plastic covers on those convenient, paper ones.

Are there other veiled losses?

Velcro removed the need to tie shoes— a skill that I was excited to acquire. Writing in cursive repeated my elation. Digital clocks have trivialized the skill of *telling time*, which is now parroted. In my long trudge to adulthood these milestones were important. Some lament that kids have it *too easy today*. I lament that kids have lost benchmarks. Such skills, though trivial to adults, are gone.

And with them, have vanished chances for small successes— at mastery.

Material changes have forever demanded amendments to the culture. In the 16th century, the style of houses was altered by the invention of the printing press—reading books required solitary spaces. And to accommodate this new pastime petitioned rooms in homes appeared. In the 20th century greeting cards, once designed by senders, became commercial. The invention of the telephone brought on the demise of personal letter writing. So writing skills, as shown on standardized tests and in employers' complaints, have decreased. Garments and linens are no longer mended—they're replaced. Mass production shattered the ancient craft of quilt making a century ago.

But quilt making has now been salvaged from the losses column. Signaling a *slow down* sign in the twenty-first century American culture. And the revival has shaken that timesaver-convenience mentality. Making a quilt takes time. Though now lacking the earlier need for survival, quilters are lured to this ancient craft of creating works of beauty from *scraps*—for the joy of mastery. Even the nibs on fountain pens can now be repaired. With all of those cheap, ballpoint pens around, real fountain pen users ignore the inconvenience of inking their pens. Hoping to achieve some personal style.

Maya Lin, creator of the Vietnam Memorial, known as The Wall in Washington, DC has taken a stance on this matter of loss. *We don't allow things to grow old today,* she notes. Her comments raise awareness of a distain for aging that can also be seen in American youth who grow up quickly—and then choose to appear twenty-five for the rest of their lives through Botox treatments. Lin's attitude is reflected in her recent, and by choice last, memorial. Located in San Francisco, the memorial is dedicated to endangered and extinct species. Where animal sounds, which we *will someday miss*, can be heard.

Lucky for us, one of the oldest living animals on the planet, the horseshoe crab, is half a billion years old. These creatures appear to have mastered their environment and would be missed— for sentimental as well as commercial reasons. A rare compound exists in the blood of horseshoe crabs, and scientists aren't able to duplicate it even in modern labs. The substance identifies contaminants in drugs and medical devices and is considered invaluable to humans. Before rushing to the dumpster with that old stuff, best we search out its worth — in our psyches.

ORACLE OF DELPHI

I often consulted my crystal ball as a kid. I knew it was a toy, but the sphere filled with a black, foreboding liquid held me in awe. I held it in my hands and asked questions, those important to a ten year old. Answers floated to the surface on tiny cards with crisp phrases such as "chances are good": "not this time": "definitely yes." Thinking back, I'm not sure how seriously I took those forecasts, but this desire to snatch a glimpse of the future hardly limits itself to kids. Searching the likes of pollster and prophet holds a hope of glimpsing the future. Knowing those scary parts suggests that matters might be changed—or at least surprises shrunk. But in reflection, my life has been anything but predictable.

On my twenty-eighth birthday, I would never have predicted that I'd move to New England. Before my next birthday. That I would raise my two young children in a state that I knew nothing about: the tiny state of Vermont. I had never been to *any* state in New England, let alone one whose entire population was half a million, whose area was 25,000 square miles— with a density of 20 people per square mile. Where, only a short time before I moved there, the cows outnumbered the people. I had grown up in Northern Virginia, a suburb of Washington, DC, the polar opposite of my destination. The population of *Northern* Virginia is three times that of the entire state of Vermont, and its density was then over a 100 people per square mile.

Until I moved to Vermont I'd never seen traffic stopped on main roadways, at any times of the day so that a herd of cows could cross. Before my move, I knew three things about this tiny state; it produced maple syrup: had less people than any other state in New England and had outstanding fall foliage. Nice information but far from comforting to a prospective resident. With less than two months to pack and prepare— to pack my clothes and prepare my emotions. I had no time for research. Between motherhood and a professional job at the time, I had just reached balance in my life. I was happy in my life in Northern Virginia.

Now with the helpful hand of hindsight, I'm glad that I didn't know what I was in for—that the experience was unpredictable. Had I known months ahead and had had time to carefully consider the giant step, I'd have found many reasons *not* to move. The move meant a big change in both climate and culture. It meant living in an area where in the beginning I would literally know no one. Uncertainty and unemployment: a couple of big un's shadowed my future. I'd be raising my kids no longer surrounded by an extended family: in fact 550 miles from them. Predictions of happiness in the strange state would have been naive at best.

Helped along by technology, prediction has become big business in the 21st century. Including scientific fields such as Western medicine. Sophisticated devices have science's approval, and now there are machines that scan entire bodies, foretelling the possibility of future illness. The sex of a baby is determined long before birth —solving the old baby shower question of pink or blue. In fact some future health issues can be solved in utero. The human, genetic code and DNA forecast outcomes of the coupling of one set of genes with another's. Tests that call for chances of contracting particular diseases abound. In fact, the majority of future ailments can now be foretold. At birth.

Writers, with a different set of tools, offer their own forecasts for the future. Their tales are woven with the power of observation—not technology. Focusing on emotional change, classics such as *Brave New World* of the thirties, followed forty years latter by *Future Shock* and eventually *Never Let Me Go,* herald dramatic changes in culture. The books' prophecies of cloning, robots, materialism and cleanliness are now reality. But writers' forecasts around emotional losses remain unsettled. As well as unsettling. The ebbing of human passion and solitary activities: the increase of feelings of impermanence: the disposability of human life are described as *likely*—an adjective that writers, not scientists, employ.

Prediction is far from new. Three thousand years ago in the ancient city of Delphi in Greece, public officials and private citizens consulted an oracle who reportedly prophesied in the name of the god Apollo. Delphi became known as the *center of the earth*— because of the aura created by the prophet. America's *Old Farmer's Almanac* has been making annual predictions for a long time, *useful* stuff for farmers and the outdoorsy folks. This yearning to know future weather can now be found in twenty-four hour television forecast— with its own channel. Weather predictions for anywhere in the world can be heard nearly anywhere in the world.

But weather predictions are safer than ones about people. More apt to be correct.

Some happenings have left us baffled. The unpredictable. America's 911 stands out among such failures. Not surprising, the most requested book *after* the attacks was *Centuries.* Written 450 years ago, the book contains famous prophecies. Readers yearned for reassurance, that *somewhere* the horror of that day in early September of 2001 had been foreseen, that clues had merely been missed along the way—a reassuring hope.

And what of scandals and assassinations? The AIDS epidemic bewildered the experts in the early eighties. And who would have predicted *two* impeachments hearings of U.S. Presidents in a twenty-five year period of American history? (Richard Nixon resigned in 1974 before the articles of impeachment were voted upon, but the votes were there. And Bill Clinton was impeached in 1998.) Impeachment of a President hadn't happened since 1868 when Andrew Johnson was impeached and then like Clinton acquitted. Another shocking item of political history was Harry Truman's leadership. Seasoned politicians who considered Truman's resume' in the light of nuclear war warned of his future failures. And were wrong. History has now ruled Truman among the ten best.

Downplaying prediction, the American Stock Market's puts a fire wall around themselves by declaring that *past performance is not an indicator of future success.* But such assertions are not found in child rearing books where poor performance in early life is often taken as a predictor of future success. Had forecasters made predictions based on the early lives of three historical figures— they would have erred embarrassingly. These stars of history had difficult starts in lives, but their childhoods failed to frame their futures. Aborting their early schooling for different reasons, all three held dim prospects. One was raised by a critical grandmother who made the decision not to send the *shy* child to elementary school. The second, who didn't speak until age three and was considered a *discipline* problem in school, dropped out at age fifteen. And the third, diagnosed as *mentally ill*, was withdrawn from school by attending adults. The adult lives of Eleanor Roosevelt, Albert Einstein, and Alexander Graham Bell, with these early, negative labels defy prediction. These giants fostered inner directions that can't be factored into forecast.

Before 1954, a forecast had been that *no* athlete could run a mile in less than four minutes. Since the four-minute mile had stood unbroken for many years, it became a *fact* that humans were physically unable to accomplish the feat. Young at the time of the famous race, I took no notice of the fanfare when Roger Bannister broke this record. I gave no thought to competitive running or records of any kind. Bannister's win was a mere *six tenths of a second* shorter than the previous, long-standing record, hardly awe-inspiring to me. But he overthrew a fact, and the unpredictable occurred. Roger Bannister achieved the *im*possible.

Bannister also increased possibilities for future runners. He had had to train without reflection on the *fact* that his goal had been deemed impossible—by experts. Once broken, his new record lasted a mere two months. Another powerful soul ran it in a second less. Without the same mental hurdle as his predecessor, the new winner had an easier task. When heeded, forecasts cause us to stand differently in the present, changing the odds where it matters most. In our minds. The odds of *one chance in a hundred* doesn't build my confidence. I don't see myself as that one person minority who can break a record. Predictions are hard to ignore. If I'm working on any sort of puzzle, it becomes easier for me to solve if I know that it's been done before.

I end as I began with my time in the tiny state of Vermont, where I abruptly moved over forty years ago. And never left. It proved an unpredictable life treasure. Biologist Lewis Thomas warns: *Most of all, we need to preserve the absolute unpredictability and total improbability of our connected minds. That way we can keep open all of the options, as we have in the past.* The unpredictable aligns with our mysterious human natures and merits attention. An inquisitive bunch, humans are armed with intuition, directions and determination. And this desire to know the future is likely those intuitions clamoring for credit. Our tools can measure the weather but not those curious inner directions. Predictions *about* us require a dash of doubt.

LIGHT ON THE CHICKEN
SOUP, PLEASE!

I was puzzled by the Martha Stewart phenomena that began in the eighties. Lots of things puzzle me, but this seemed bigger. Her stamp now graces books, magazines, home goods and a TV show. Her stock has soared. Time devoted to the creation of a comfortable home yields its own reward. No argument here. But her methods are time-consuming and expensive—in this age of convenience. Even the craft people among us would have trouble achieving a table covered with their own crocheted tablecloth, flaunting homemade gourmet food and a centerpiece in a ceramic vase baked in their own kiln— filled with flowers grown in the backyard. Focusing on the comforts of home delivers feelings of security, but Martha's promoting more than a happy home here. And until I know what's really selling, I'm not buying.

I can engage an expert to do just about anything these days. Surrounded by specialists, I can get a skilled one to do the job quickly. Leaving flowers to the gardener: cooking to the caterers: pottery to the craftspeople and crocheting—well, to the dexterous among us. Specialists study a lot about a narrow field. And in the 21st century there are more of them than ever, ones unheard of twenty years ago: exotic fields of lactation, relational disorders, elder law, sleep disorders. On and on. Now there are experts who can *fix* human bodies through cosmetic and gender surgery. Why should I aim for status as a jack-of-all-trades in an age where work can be delegated? The specialist gifts me time for other pursuits as well as the assurance of their skill.

Still, such authorities make me feel helpless. I start to question myself. Do I know enough to undertake—anything? I feel the scary cloak of dependence.

Dependence showed up on my inner screen through the life of a beloved aunt who entered a nursing home at age eighty-two. It was a good facility that met her physical needs. Without effort or input from her, she had three hot, nutritious meals a day, was clean, safe and secure. All of the time. But she wasn't the woman I had known my whole life. She no longer smiled. Life's allure, which had forever steered her course, had vanished. Living an active, adult life that began at age sixteen when her father died before his time, my aunt went to work to help her immigrant mother feed five, younger children. Working as a seamstress, she paid her way through cosmetology school, bought and ran her own shop until she was forty-five years old—when she finally sold her business and married. There had been lots of boyfriends, but only now did she decide to make a commitment. Menopause had set in, and she likely felt that she had earned an early retirement, finally a *pause* in her life. Life still excited her, though not the housewife role.

She had traveled even during her working years. Now at forty-five, married and retired, she and her husband increased their travel. She loved the thrill of new places and new ideas—and the risks that went along with them. Gambling, and the risks it carried, became important: horse races: slot machines and poker at the tables of Les Vegas. The two traveled at every chance. After a busy, thirty-seven year retirement and his death, she entered the nursing home.

When I visited her, she struggled to convince me that life was fine. Depression had never been her style of being in the world—her modus operandi. Now in the nursing home, no insight of hers brought on more than a courteous smile from attendants. Of sound mind, she soon learned that her opinions and judgments no longer mattered, were no longer sought. Dependent and powerless in this stagnant environment, she was doomed long before her physical ailments completed the job.

Happy endings aren't always possible. *Happily ever after* ends fairy tales not real life. So I'll add a bit of *if only* to her story. If only she could have spent those last five years as a senior guide, a docent, in a museum of some sort. She'd have been questioned and empowered by visitors if she could have shared her big life. Instead of seeing it all vanish in the atmosphere of the nursing home—where workers faithfully did their jobs: to keep her alive. As in previous parts of her life, the decision to go to the nursing home was her own. Probably the last flicker of independence in her life.

Such independence can't be expressed by the captive species of the planet. Who land in zoos and have keepers, just as did my aunt. Zoo habitats are environmentally correct these days, and the animals, studied by resident zoologists, are fed precisely what they require—at the right time of day. Such a setup seems ideal. The animals are no longer prey for other species and don't spend their days forging for food. Other than appealing to audiences on the other side of the bars, nothing is expected of these captives. Capable of making decisions based on pure instinct in the wild, zoo animals are dependent. Their survival no longer rests on their judgments.

But life in the zoo doesn't meet the vital litmus test. Nature has trouble replicating in captivity. Only on rare occasions does breeding happen. And that only with much human intervention. Evolution dictates survival of the fittest, and evidently Nature doesn't view caged animals as sufficiently fit to reproduce. Nor do animals in captivity achieve their normal life span. Captive creatures probably sense their uselessness to the life force, as my aunt did, and lose that vital will to survive.

Similar to zoos are Indian reservations. Generous efforts are made by the U.S. Federal Government to supply a familiar way of life for the American Indian. But the dependent residents of these encampments turn to alcohol and more recently serious gambling—to pass the day. Neither action implies much satisfaction. Inhabitants of nursing homes, zoos and reservations make few judgment calls of their own.

It's that nagging feeling of dependence in all of us that sells Martha Stewart today.

Martha's *from scratch* recipes suggest that skill, not convenience, is required. I really *can* do many of those things that I've turned over to the specialists— if only I had the time. On popular, reality TV shows, people struggle with hurdles that don't exist in modern times, to prove their independence. Stripped of all convenience, just as they are in Martha's world, participants of these shows attempt to prove that they're independent of modernity and all its perks. That *their* judgments are still important. These shows are repeated in a variety of challenging settings: the Australian Outback and the American Frontier— as they existed four hundred years ago. Impressing on audiences that they are not aiding the contestants, directors still run interference in chancy situations and supply safety nets for participants—liability is an issue. The shows are likely staged, but this matters not. It's only the messages to the audiences that count.

I admit that I do cave to dependence when it comes to politics. I depend on the politicians who got my vote. I have no interest in the infrastructure of cities outside my travel zone or in the endless mediations necessary in foreign policy. Ronald Reagan instinctively knew that most voters were like me, anxious to be rescued from political minutiae. Described by historians as a political specialist, Reagan communicated to voters that they could depend on him. Promising in campaigns that *he* would restore the country's glory. Reagan asked nothing of citizens—who gladly complied. Before his presidency, Reagan was a lifeguard and later attempted to rid the country of Communists in the film industry. He *rescued* people. Claiming freedom for voters, he was elected by landslides for two terms—and would have likely stayed in office had the Twenty-second Amendment not limited the presidential term. With Reagan's message, little was required of the voters who depended on him. Reagan ran for the first time in 1980 and defeated Jimmy Carter who had called for sacrifice by citizens. Voters chose Reagan over Carter because they preferred the cushy job: Reagan's advice. *"Keep America great by honoring the flag."*

Spiritual figures have urged independence. Both Jesus and Buddha told followers to be independent of them: to perhaps follow their lessons but not to venerate the teachers. Both teachers discouraged their followers from idolizing them. Less concerned with spiritual leanings, Ralph Waldo Emerson wrote "we must walk on our own two feet —work with our own hands and speak our own minds. Emerson, part of the Transcendental movement of the mid-nineteenth century recommended that we humans follow our intuitions, not social mores.

The first cry for independence comes from two-year-olds. Barely making sentences, these toddlers manage the same, simple sentence: *No. I do it myself.* The Terrible Twos became famous in the fifties when Dr Spock coined it. But the period is only terrible for parents who get wearied by the constant cries for independence from their two-year-olds. These little ones have little knowledge of danger so their demands for self-rule have limits, but their insistence carries an inborn message. Which looks to be fading fast in modern times.

I doubt that Nature planned that the Terrible Twos' cry for independence would evaporate over time. It was meant to increase so that new ideas could pierce the culture. Even in the spiritual realm, the task can't be farmed out. Huston Smith our present house scholar on religion is forever questioned about how one would choose when the world religions are so similar. Smith writes that the spiritual journey is a solitary one. One that can't be made by theologians, the experts in this field. Surrounded in the twenty-first century by the convenience and abundance of expert advice, I plan to saddle my own horse for as long as I can— at least to *know how* to do it.

SCHOOL DAZE

I no longer worry that the *back to school* sales in early August will eventually imitate Christmas shopping, which now begins before the Halloween candy is gone. That push to buy school supplies for the return to school creeps in a bit earlier each year—the buying event that now trips on the heels of July Fourth. But convincing parents to buy school supplies *before* school closes in June is doubtful. Even for the merchants. When school openings are flashed in sales events, I hear winter's whistle. The ads herald summer's demise and warn of winter. School openings divide summer and winter more clearly than the official, fall equinox in late September. In America, the toll of the school bell is a *back to business* signal, silencing summer's spirit of play. Whether school connection is tight or faint, life changes when that bell rings.

Serious business is flagged by the return of the yellow school bus and explains why year-round schools have never garnered gusto in America. Twelve month schools, as exists in other countries, have been studied extensively here—and forever abandoned. The casualness of life ends when school resumes. For everyone. Vacations, poolsides and outdoor activities fade. Summer action movies end, and an earnest march to the year's Academy Awards begins. TV drops all reruns to delivers their new shows.

A line between winter and summer divides work and play in America.

Sociologist Phillip Slater writes that Americans, more than citizens of other countries, don't allow themselves *natural* play. Slater writes, "Americans find it necessary to *build* playgrounds," implying an odd need to erect something that flows naturally—when allowed. Play is a free and normal part of humanness, not restricted to children, Slater declares. *Natural* traits, like smiling, don't require green lights. Americans seem to need permission to play, to relax. (A consent too often gained with alcohol or drugs.) That old Pilgrims' motto: "the devil finds use for idle hands" lingers, entering even the design of American schools. Where kids do school*work*. The novelty of those initial days of school in the early fall, with new teachers and lapsed friendships to renew, fades quickly for kids. The new lunchbox, sharpened pencils and colorful notebooks soon lose their luster. Leaving kids with only schoolwork. They trudge to school with excitement in their wake—and work ahead of them for the next nine months.

Childhood, that period in all cultures before formal schooling begins, is a time when work and play are one. Governed by Nature, learning is fun *and useful* in those first few years of life. In those times, kids play and learn— at the same time. Open-ended toys, logs, blocks, and Tinker Toys, those without defined goals, allow for meandering minds. Nature supplies the motivation through kids' egocentric natures and delivers crucial confidence. In this solitary process of childhood, matters of physics are learned: up, down, gravity, stress, balance, dexterity and finally walking and running. All of this is achieved with neither school nor teachers. Or well-meaning adults trying to *make* learning enjoyable.

Recognizing this gloom about school as work, educators have tried for the last forty years to follow the words of the seer Mary Poppins: *a spoonful of sugar makes the medicine go down.* Thus the goal has been to *build* fun into learning for students. Just like those planned playgrounds of which Slater writes. The extreme example of such efforts arrived in American schools with the revision of the classic story of "The Elves and the Shoemaker." The old tale was adapted for six-year-olds by reducing the vocabulary of the story to what was considered a *suitable* level for this age. Elf and shoemaker became banned words. So of course the tale's title had to change. The ancient fairytale was renamed "Tap, Tap,

Tap." The process, eventually labeled *dumbing down,* has now been abandoned.

But this goal to *make learning fun* continues. And might be reached if kids could learn subject matter through computer programs. Original in many ways, these games are advertised as head *starts* for each grade level and are available to anyone. Entertaining for those early years, the games have fishes juggling numbers: antelopes explaining their terrain: ships sailing through the intestines: hotels on the planets of the solar system: mere cats eating mosaic bugs: warthogs hanging from vines: hyenas playing xylophones. Excitement at every turn. When wrong answers are given, the programs nobly try not to discourage young learners. Though fun to play with such colorful images on screens that have become common to kids, the isolated answers are facts and figures— without context.

Modern tools such as graphing calculators: portable spell-checks, in different languages: Wikipedia and audio-visuals of all sorts are available through the high school years. All aimed at making learning fun. Not work. Teachers struggle to enhance lessons with more videos, but the visual, so much a part of kids' daily lives, usually leaves them, in their words, "bored."

Those well-meaning flourishes have failed. The high school dropout rate across the public schools in the U. S. has risen to 30 percent. In the Global Education Ranking of 2012, Finland ranked #1, and the U.S. ranked #17. These ugly facts were beginning to seep through in surveys done in 2006 but are now public. Since schooling is mandated in most states until age sixteen, most dropouts aren't of the legal age of 18 so are minors when they leave the halls of learning. But when students choose to terminate their formal schooling, parents know a losing battle— drive is gone.

I've lived a total of thirty-two public school openings in my professional career. I was being paid for going to work while kids were not being paid— for going to work, or so they reminded me. Ten of my years were spent in elementary schools and the other twenty-two in high schools. Spending twice as much time with the older kids, I heard many, well-worded complaints from their end of the field. The younger ones were happier and didn't complain as much. Elementary schools still had playgrounds for recess breaks. Kids are eager to start kindergarten, but by the time puberty sets in, they're wildly searching for that adult self, making schoolwork extraneous.

As a high school counselor in the eighties, I tired of complaints around class schedules. Changes in these took up most of the month of September, 10 percent of the school year. Given the size of the real bumps in the road they'd face in the future, my time and theirs felt wasted on these unpopular schedules. During the period, I found a teachable moment—a chance where work could be turned to play. Profitable play, when a student's effort proved enjoyable— and beneficial. Known as arena scheduling, the process was far from new; colleges had used it for years. But American public high schools had been reluctant to use such a process because of local budgets. In public schools, the number of classes, courses and teachers remained unknown until the budget passed each year.

With arena scheduling, the students, rather than computers, create their class schedule for the oncoming year. Not necessarily one they love but a compromise that they make and can live with for a school year. Students (ages fourteen to seventeen) fit their chosen courses and teachers into limited spaces. As in a jigsaw puzzle, they come up with a schedule of their own creation. It may not be their ideal one, but they've made alternate choices—a bit like life itself. In the three high schools amply courageous to try this approach, I saw empowered kids as I had never seen before. Kids who learned decision-making skills and collected a direct payoff. I watched them ask questions of teachers about unknown courses as they learned for the first time the kinship between departments in the school. With this new bird's-eye view, teens felt more linked to the school system. Aerial outlooks are always useful. Knowing the whole picture of anything, rather than isolated close-ups, forever empowers through connections and shortcuts.

But the powerful computer can't be ignored in the twenty-first century so class schedules in public high schools today are formally run with all kinds of new programs. Computers are easier and faster—than high school kids. But in this rush to make everything quick and convenient in this twenty-first century, human nature is overlooked. Fortunately, good teachers still offer courses that encourage analysis of popular movies, television commercials and current news events that empower kids by building critical thinking around the concrete stuff. Once involved, kids slide with little effort into abstract studies.

For the 70 percent who earn a high school diploma in America, graduation night in some school districts includes a program called Project Graduation. This nationally known program, begun in the mid-eighties with the intention of keeping graduates *safe,* is an alcohol-free affair and evolved because commencement was too often celebrated with excessive alcohol. Which led to car fatalities. Project Graduation encourages community businesses to donate food and activities so that the graduates can stay out all night—and stay sober. High school graduates, mostly eighteen, are of *legal age of consent* for everything except alcohol.

Twelve years of school hasn't taught responsible judgment?

Leapfrog, Hop Scotch, Jump Rope, Hide and Seek, Kick the Can—like tree climbing, all are shaped by kids and surpass the structured playgrounds that will never hold such excitement. The human brain seeks stimulation, and we're hardwired for play. Combined, those two facts and the accomplishments of the building-block years could serve as a model for formal education. Only thoughts separate work and play: and detach learning from fun. Maybe with this simple alignment, it will be easier to empower those brainy adolescents.

ONLY CHILD'S PLAY

I was never advised to use my imagination as a kid. Following on the heels of two world wars, a stock market crash, and the Great Depression, the times held little incentive for flights of fancy. Only practical topics delivered the security that era required. *Normalcy* was its pressing goal. A dutiful kid, I never questioned cultural conventions. I didn't know where the rules came from in the first place so occasionally dragged my feet. But most of the time, I followed the rules as I heard them, as well as those I learned through osmosis. Some were vague and harder to get straight. A word like *imagination* carried a double meaning and was confusing to a kid like me. *You have quite an imagination* might mean that I was creative, a positive—or delusional: a negative. So which is it?

I'm quick to declare that one of my friends had an imagination, and in her case it was a definite plus. Mary's mom brought home wallpaper to spruce up her bedroom when Mary was a five-year-old who knew few of the rules. (Such rules are known by lots of names: cultural customs: mutual mores: social rules.) When presented with the wallpaper, Mary was soon smitten by the hardened glue on the *wrong* side of the wallpaper—much more than the repeated, printed pattern on the *right* side that had captivated her mother. Mary chose the swirling, yellow glue to adorn her walls. With delicate debate, her mother met Mary's plea and covered the very prints that had attracted her. The yellow, twirling glue was displayed for the next eight years. Taken by the unusual forms of glue, Mary gave no thought to the right side of that paper—though likely her mother mourned it for a time. For Mary at age five, there existed no right or wrong in the category of wallpaper. Or anything else.

Before entering school, kids are imaginative. Nature designs them to explore a world, which they believe revolves around them. Egocentric and confident kids are primed for discovery. Mary at five wasn't unique. Her mother was the unusual one of that pair—allowing the wrong side of that paper to adorn the walls of a room in her home. As a grown-up, Mary credited her mother's attitude with her own career, eventually that of an accomplished artist. Adults might say that Mary had an *overactive* imagination. But sarcasm means little to young minds. Not positive of the rules, those under six don't always see things—the *right* way. That collective adult way.

Without effort, kids shut others out. Solitude comes naturally to them and as yet cooperation means nothing. Rudeness at the age of four is undefined in the social rule book. Even surrounded by others of the same age at daycares, kids' conversations are with themselves. Before formal schooling, they live in the moment— rather than tomorrow and yesterday. They discover unusual things to do with objects that they find in their world. They turn tricycles over, excited to now have a spinning wheel. They bang spoons on bowls, discovering to their delight that the bowl also rolls. Then they learn the *right* rules— a drumstick bangs on drums and wheels roll. And *only* those previously printed patterns on wallpaper are visible when placed on walls. While those tiny hands remain innocent, nothing has one purpose.

Innocent of social restraint, kids act on curiosity, which implies a lack of restraint. But the Zen tradition of the Tao teaches that less control results in *more* power. (Sexual orgasm, a spontaneous peak, created us all. Could there be more power than this?) Innocent of adult reality, kids aren't positive what does and doesn't exist and reach different conclusions. *My kitty talks to me when you're not around, Mom. <u>That</u> star in the sky is really mine and twinkles when I'm sad. If I make a wish with <u>this</u> stone in my hand, it will come true.*

In school, kids learn that they have to share their world. That innate imagination slips a bit when those mutual mores are learned. It becomes harder to ignore the rules. A conundrum of sorts arises.

Innocence implies vulnerability so parents forever worry over their child's safety—often concluding that the many screens around even their teenagers in the twenty-first century keeps them safe. One screen or another insulates them—and keeps them out of speeding cars with drunk drivers or that wrong crowd of peers. Kids in front of screens are safe and stationary. Inactivity among mammals for safety reason isn't new and has been a survival device for millions of years. Neither the largest nor strongest of the planet, humans who are motionless improve their changes of survival. Squirrels immediately freeze when they sense the presence of another species. And we have neither the camouflage nor the agility of that little rodent.

So what happens to that childish imagination?

Though my imagination doesn't flow as it once did, when I failed to appreciate it, I still visualize images in my mind. The images now are translated to words that I've learned. I write when I wander within to that creative part of my mind. But I'm distracted these days by the many screens on the many gadgets. There are screens for movies: television: cell phones: Internet: i-Pads, GPSs: video games: DVDs: digital cameras. On and on. All devices direct attention to achieve a specific goal. Gadgets, like habits, demand that tasks be completed in a fixed manner. Habits *are* "fixed manners" which is why young kids have few if any of them—they have few specific goals. My computer is programmed to shorten my tasks, and the commanding voice on the popular Global Positioning System (GPS) directs my journey to assure that I reach a planned destination. And for added certainty, the trip is tracked on a screen—though viewing it while driving is discouraged. Habits and gadgets reject those winding sideroads that just might sidetrack me and lead to mental meanderings. Reverie.

Bob Dylan meandered within when he wrote and set to music his soul-searching words. Likely, a music teacher would have instructed him to improve his voice — or stick to writing poetry. But Dylan knew that the sixties were ripe for song so he began to *sing* his words. For circulation, his imaginative message had to be in musical not written form. Dylan's creativity lies in his prose, his music *and* his method of delivery. Though it's his music that made him famous, Dylan is now known as the *poet* of the twentieth century. And I've never heard it claimed that he had an *overactive imagination*.

Inventors meander in their minds. At first, they roam without a defined destination. *Possibilities* not programs are their fodder. It's messy in the beginning—no one wants to be around for that first part of the process: when rules and ridicule have to be ignored. Eventually some inventor will come along and pull in the two senses missing from gadgets today: smell and taste. With its amazing ability to retrieve memories, smell may be the most difficult. And that geek won't find a program that offers directions. Everything in the physical world has already been invented. By someone night dreams are imaginative vehicles. Those screens, no longer of use, disappear when asleep. Noteworthy inventors of the sewing machine: periodic tables of chemistry: molecular structure of the benzene ring, and quantum theory all claim to have had dreams that *directed* their eventual discovery. Dreams come from within us, fracturing most of the rules—or at least bending them. All bets are off in the dream state. Dreams permit amazing acts of flying and bilocation. Paradox of all sorts happens when time and place no longer confine the dreamer. In dreams, events casually unfold without misgiving, offering new perspectives that can be translated and refined in the waking hours. In dreams, items don't have a specific use.

In an experiment on perception, volunteers were given a box containing a variety of items, which included necessary as well as needless objects to complete a task. Those who were successful had to imagine the box that *held* the supplies differently. Boxes and bags are containers with a specific use, and it's difficult for those beyond school age to see them otherwise. The box itself was needed to complete the assignment and couldn't be disregarded. Those who didn't see it as something they could put to use failed the assignment.

Like all inventors, Louis C Tiffany first needed to digest facts about his world. As a young man, he studied the stained glass windows of the Middle Ages, which were painted and etched with a variety of acids— generally for cathedral windows. In the middle of the nineteenth century, this was considered the most that could be done with this substance known as glass. Tiffany's mental meanderings rejected the centuries old definition of stained glass— he broke a few rules. Making glass could be more than a skill, more could be done with this substance, he concluded. Traveling on those sideroads, inventors get willful. Finally, Tiffany saw glass as an art form and left behind iridescent glass lamps and vases— new objects he called "opalescent." Seventy-five years after his death, *Tiffany* glass is priceless. (Well, for me it is.)

Bob Dylan sang his poetry with a scratchy voice. Tiffany insisted that art could be useful and decorative, not just museum pieces. And my friend Mary got an early start with hardened glue. Encouraging more meandering on the *wrong* side might empower more of their kind. And before kids learn all the rules, maybe we can learn a thing or two from them.

RISKY BUSINESS

I once planned to one day rest on my laurels. Pondering the *golden years*, I banked on basking in a state of minimum effort: the status quo. Then I read a study of nursing home residents that concluded that longevity resulted from novelty and risk taking. *Risk* taking in nursing homes? The nursing home study followed the scientific model and can't be lightly dismissed. There were two groups in the study; the experimental group made decisions on their own while the control group had caregivers choosing for them— keeping them safe by deciding when activities were unfit. These caretakers decided the degree of risk for those who were spectators in their own lives. The study concluded that when residents of the homes were forced to make choices, they lived longer. Nor does it end here. The *riskier* the choice, the better the results. Residents lived even longer. Finally, the participants who stretched their comfort levels and had less predictable outcomes lived the longest. I guess that it can be argued that there's less to lose in those twilight years, but risk taking at ninety seems a bit of a stretch to me.

Pondering this question of risk, I quickly shelved those between the ages of thirteen and twenty-five. Emboldened with those young strong bodies that suggest immortality, most in this age group are fearless and discard even the sensible safety rules. Such risks as unprotected sex, fraternity hazings and speeding cars while under influence of— well, a variety of things— confirm recent findings. Research in brain development concludes that the human brain does not fully develop and sound decision-making doesn't occur until the *late* twenties. Research shows that until then, teens can't predict the consequences of their behavior. Simply put, this age group can't accurately predict the consequences of their behavior. And are invalid risk takers.

I took a big risk when I once quit a secure job— without the assurance of a replacement. The year was 1976, and Jimmy Carter had just been elected President of the United States. Carter was an unknown: a peanut farmer from Georgia with spiritual leanings, who was elected seemingly beholden to no political cronies. It was the same year that America celebrated its bicentennial of independence from England. America seemed to have freed itself in more ways than one that year. A spirit of independence enveloped the country. And I caught the mood. I resigned my job of seven years with an air of liberation, ignoring data such as a high jobless rate and low starting salaries at the time. Though I trusted the huge decision, I was soon filled with the kind of anxiety that isn't easily forgotten. After a year's search I finally found a good job and quickly vowed to avoid such risky behavior in the future.

But seven years later, with both Jimmy Carter and the two hundredth anniversary long forgotten, I neglected my vow and again walked away from a viable job— again without the assurance of another one. Since I had survived the first risk with minimal scars, the act became easier for me. After only a small search this time around, I became gainfully employed. And remained so for the next five years until I took my third risk— and resigned again without the safety net of a new job. This time, I was so confident that I even prepared for the possibility of a period of joblessness. My planning improved, and I made permanent living arrangements where I hoped to settle into a new job. After all, I had survived scary outcomes of serious job searches twice before. By the third time, I'd gained momentum in building my confidence. I got a job in less than a month— and bought a house in the city, before the offer. My earlier practice shots had trained me.

Practice shots count. They improve just about anything by shrinking the consequences— and building confidence. Risk recedes with rehearsal. But when the goal changes, more practice may be in order. The choice of a fifty mile bike ride would require a different kind of risk than job hunting for me. Far riskier for me than such a choice made by a Tour de France rider. Even one without steroids.

Midst the convenience of life in twenty-first century America, consequences have faded. With twenty-four hour weather coverage, the chance of not being prepared for a storm—windows down, no umbrella—is unlikely. With ATM machines: automatic deposits: twenty-four hour stores and the Internet, it's almost impossible to be shutout of transactions because of poor planning. Making technical *business hours* moot. I can bank and buy anything now at any hour Online. Banking and tickets of all sorts can be carried out Online, instead of standing *in* line. Thus avoiding the cheerless phrase *sold-out* or *overdrawn* after effortful acts such as speeding to the theater or struggling with checkbooks. Planning and cooking the evening meal can be reduced to a last minute run to the grocery store. Cell phones and microwaves allow for last minute measures that eliminate all sorts of frustration. And all sorts of consequences.

But why lament the loss of painful consequences? As long as they aren't deadly, unwanted outcomes train us, argued Austrian psychologist Alfred Adler at the beginning of the twentieth century. He insisted that since dire consequences are memorable, future decisions are better. And build confidence. A medical doctor and colleague of the more famous Sigmund Freud, Adler encouraged parents to allow for hurtful (not dangerous) outcomes in their children's choices. He labeled consequences *natural learning devices* and advised that kids be allowed to endure the price of poor choices; toys that are not cared for aren't replaced. Laundry, not in the assigned basket, isn't washed. When troubles arise in kids' peer relationships, anxious parents don't fix them. It seems that convenience wasn't Adler's goal. Adjusted kids who eventually became powerful adults were.

Adler argued that by enduring the consequences of their actions, kids come to trust their decisions. This in turn allows them to assume more risk as adults. The kind of healthy risks that extend comfort zones. (The kind of risks taken by the nursing home residents who lived the longest.) Adler warned that those deprived of consequences would suffer and become "emotional cripples" as adults— strong words of warning. Writing a hundred years ago, before the technology explosion, Adler knew nothing of modern gadgets or of science's warnings of danger.

It's risky to breathe these days. Even what we inhale has been declared dangerous; air could contain: lead, asbestos, radon, mold, carbon monoxide, free radicals. And a poor choice at the wrong time could deliver: PMS, SIDS, CFS, PTS, PPD, SARS. (These abbreviated forms of dangers make it easier to commit to memory, and by occupying less space, acronyms allow for new ones to follow.) Then there is cholesterol: bipolar disorder (recently broadened to include children as young as three), random shootings: food dye: Reye Syndrome: reflux disorder: e-coli: pesticides: Lyme and Mad Cow Diseases: Bird Flu: Swine Flu: On and on. The carcinogenic list alone carries 218 suspects. Prescription drugs, the dominant television ad today, claim to protect us from many of these physical dangers. Such knowledge may help some, but they also foment fear and reawaken my survival needs.

Fear and doubt over physical safety linger, though it's no longer about the large animals for whom humans once were dinner. Now we fear each other. Burglars, rapists, pedophiles, terrorists harbor evil intentions and possess destructive tools, my psyche warns. Then there's nuclear war, AIDs, and the possibility of germ warfare. No training ground for practice shots and warning labels attached to so many things? New choices feel riskier today than in the past, greatly increasing that spectator group.

Members of the control group in that nursing home study were spectators who didn't participate in their lives. But not all spectators require caregivers, nor do they reside in nursing homes. Merely members of an audience, bystanders are ageless and can be found anywhere. Anytime. Sitting on bleachers, excited by those who perform in life's arena, spectators *observe*. Living vicarious lives, they find excitement through the lives of others and remain in the grandstands. Spectators account for the growing numbers of celebrity-watchers today who hanker for even a picture of popular idols. The more intimate the photo, the higher the paparazzi's price. Under such demand, superstars have a shorter road to fame. Becoming a superstar requires less time— and little talent. Consider: Bristol Palin: Paris Hilton: Lady Gaga and Justin Bieber. My view.

Training to take risks comes naturally, before assisted living is necessary. Philosopher Sam Keen avoided the role of spectator first as author of well-known books such as *Fire in the Belly*, where he writes of strong men who admit that war scares them. Even more personal, Keen tried for the first time a stint as a trapeze artist— at the age of sixty-two. He had been fascinated by circus acts since childhood and finally decided to fulfill a personal dream. At an advanced age, he literally stepped off the bleachers of the circus tent and took a risk as he swung through the air with a far less nimble body than the twenty-year-olds who surrounded him.

Had Keen been in the control group of that nursing home study undoubtedly the trapeze is not a choice a caretaker would have made for him. Though his high wire act demotes the kind of chances taken by even the daringest of residents in the nursing home study, both the experimental group and Keen took risks that will likely extend their lives. I'm not sure I would have tried the high wire even as that teenager—whom science now claims can't predict the outcome of her choices. My nature cowers at the trapeze, but with a safety net under me, I'd consider it. To avoid those bleachers.

PRACTICALLY PERFECT

I was forced to read Plato's *Republic* at some point in school. As do most students, I wondered why. What effect could a book written thousands of years ago have on *my* life in twenty-first century America? But as I thought of such things as government, social rules and the culture that enveloped me, I appreciated the Greek philosopher's goal. Plato had a blueprint for an ideal civilization that went beyond simple survival. One that was moral and met the needs of its citizens. Such a social order can't be bashed and became the vision of thinkers who followed him. After five thousand years of civilization and the invention of some amazing tools, do we live in a perfect civilization? Are we there yet?

Plato wrote his classic book about four hundred years before the birth of Jesus. The Greek city-state in which he taught is seen as the great-grandparent of modern democracy. Plato suggests three classes of people: leaders, soldiers, and civilians. Simple and clear. He advises that the leaders *receive* intellectual training and exercise political power in the service of justice. These leaders are the philosophers, of which of course Plato was one. The second group known as soldiers protects the state and thus acquire honor. And finally the civilians provide for the material needs of the society. Thus, Plato's formula for a perfect civilization— in ninety-four words.

A perfect civilization? An endgame where no more changes happen?

I had no thoughts of riding a two-wheeler *perfectly*, when I first learned to ride. I was eight years old and doubt that "perfect" was in my lexicon. Labeled two-wheelers at the time, they were clearly separate from the little kids' three-wheelers. One was no longer a *little kid* on a two-wheeler. Riding a two-wheeler was another one of those milestones on the trek to adulthood. Kids recorded those stepping stones. Riding a two-wheeler swelled my independence, and by the time my parents bought me one of my own, I was allowed to ride a bit further from home every day. Finally I got permission to ride to school and soon felt responsible for both me and the bike. *Times they were a'changin'.*

In high school, the two-wheeler waned for me. Suddenly there were boys, cars and college and then marriage and children to fill my life. Then bikes reappeared — this time for health and entertainment in my life. They were simple, free exercise, fun and accessible. By then, many cities were attuned to preventive medicine and built long, scenic bike paths. My goal became distance. How far could I bike? How was my endurance? Still young enough to muster the courage for a risk, I moved on to balance. Could I ride without holding the handlebars? Muscles in my legs worked harder to achieve balance when I wasn't steering with my hands, so I concluded, *this has to be good for me!* So I rode further, but knowing by then I'd never get to perfect.

Perfect is a process. There is no finish, only future feats.

So Plato's plan was a perfectly good start with plenty of room for improvement— neither women nor slaves had the right to vote in his early stab at democracy. But social orders evolve with the times, and today the material needs of civilians are different than in Plato's day. Most material needs, and some emotional ones, are provided by one unique tool unknown to the ancient philosopher.

Of course it's the computer. Life today literally unfolds at our fingertips as we interact with this amazing tool. With the aid of the World Wide Web, computers deliver: directions, research, travel, music—even socialization. They produce tickets, applications and tax forms, while allowing us to make reservations, pay bills and invest money without leaving the easy chair. Even away from home, barcodes communicate with the computer in retail—making shopping easier. Making life more convenient.

Beyond the personal, computers have enabled businesses to increase efficiency tenfold. Hospitals and doctors use them to share their diagnoses with experts across the world—eliminating the guesswork that puts life and death on the line. Science employs computers to reduce years of research and make existing studies more accessible to new studies. In addition to the serious business, computers entertain. The popularity of computer games has both hard and software in a constant state of update. Used purely for fun, these games proudly proclaim "virtual reality." Attempting to copy certain life thrills in the programs, manufacturers compete and base their ads on who gets closest to *reality*. Players capture some of the feelings behind the real actions in such risky sports as snowboarding, football, boxing, and car racing. A similar experience is delivered by High Density Television, with its *computer*ized innards. Credit for stunning armchair travel in living rooms belongs to the computer.

The personal computer is one of us. A vital presence amongst us. Such dominance distinguishes the computer from other tools. Computers carry intimate messages from loved ones through electronic mail. Facebook and Twitter, available only through computers, carry out social networking and continue to evolve. Without leaving that comfortable armchair, connections with old friends are made. Sometimes life partners are met. No society has reached a point of such accuracy, convenience, efficiency. In the 21st century, the computer occupies a revered spot in the majority of American homes. A simulated voice greets me in the morning and bids me goodnight at bedtime. Encouraging familiarity by the use of first names, computers also contract *viruses*— just as we do. Such intimacy will likely increase with time, as manufacturers recognize the advantage of such a liaison. Suggesting a coalition between me and my computer.

The missing element in this bond between me and this remarkable tool is responsibility. In the dawn of the century, I'm the accountable party of this union. Though helpful aides, computers are still only "reliable." Humans remain in charge. My computer suggests that I consider my actions: *save: delete: recycle*? Correcting my spelling and grammar, the tool automatically inserts dates and addresses. Facts can quickly be checked through the Web, but in the end errors are assigned to *me*—to my input. But in the end, if that perfect document doesn't come forth, the machine can't be blamed. The buck stops with me.

Research has been acting to change this. Working towards an artificial intelligence since the sixties, IBM did it in February of 2011. Their computer's name is Watson with artificial intelligence sufficient enough to beat a human at his own game of Jeopardy. Computer Watson also has a personality as the namesake of the Dr Watson of Sherlock Holmes fame. In the Sherlock Holmes detective stories, Dr Watson lacks the deductive reasoning of his friend the emotionally detached, famous detective Sherlock Holmes. The choice of the name Watson for the computer implies a human touch. Making Watson responsible?

Responsibility is about passion. Responsible people are passionate enough about issues to show-up and take the blame when results appear dire. *Half* the eligible voters, one hundred million people, failed to vote in the memorable Bush versus Gore 2000 election in America. Irresponsible, these nonvoters failed to show up so the final decision went to the U.S. Supreme Court. Lacking sufficient passion for even the completion of an absentee ballot, these spectators allowed the input of others to choose a world leader. Maybe they reasoned that the computer would come up with the perfect selection. After all, computers produce "ideal" matches in dating scenarios. The vote count in Florida went unresolved for a month, while the country clamored for news of a leader. The photo finish election ended when the nine Supreme Court justices made a decision that left the eerie fact that *five hundred votes*, a fraction of the nonvoters, could have determined who would become *the leader of the free world*. Nonvoters learned that their vote counted—quite a bit.

To avoid such frustration in future elections, better voting machines (computers in disguise) were immediately proposed in many states. Even the unaffected states of the country scrutinized their machines—harboring faith in well functioning computers. Better *voters* ought to have been the first goal. Rather than aim for superior voting machines, why not inspire impassioned voters? Those sufficiently responsible to at least show up with a vote.

With the help of computers that quest for the perfect civilization will continue. But even for the accountable computer of the future, responsibility and passion can't be programmed. If the task is left to the computer, such human intangibles will vanish Plato's passion viewed good citizenship as part of a happy life, but details such as the voting machine wouldn't have interested this philosopher who longed for an ideal society.

The Titanic was labeled a perfect construction—flawless, until it sank. Enthralled with the wonders of convenience, both passengers and crew of the infamous liner became passive, indifferent, and failed to heed iceberg warnings. While Noah's passion around the survival of *all* life likely kept that ark afloat. Responsibility fueled by passion gets us to show up, and taking the word of Woody Allen, *90 percent of life is about showing up.* Best we listen to a sage of our times.

PART II

SOURCES OF POWER

We habitually attribute too much to the world and not enough to ourselves.

Ralph Waldo Emerson

TIME IS OF THE ESSENCE

I was stunned in the early seventies when McDonald's added their first drive-through. Fast food became faster. Sociologists soon noted the passing of the evening meal in American family life. Then I read that most people took less time to eat *any* meal than in the past. *On the run* became a catch phrase in packaging. Still, I reasoned, I spend less time than my ancestors on lots of things. I'm delighted to wash clothes differently than my grandmother once did. Taking into account only laundry time, I have seven hours a week more freedom than she had. Adding up the hours of all those dreadful chores of the past, I'm amassing a stash of time that no doubt will increase in the future. How will all this extra time be spent?

A poor immigrant, my grandmother came here for an arranged marriage at the beginning of the 20th century. She came from Galacia, Poland, once the extreme western part of Russia. The manifest of the boat lists her as a *steerage* passenger with no luggage. Deserting her birth family at age nineteen for an arranged marriage in the new world, she had no luggage? Most of us don't make such a decision unless things are pretty bad at home. My guess is that she expected life to be easier here—instead of what she had known in the Carpathian Mountains of southwest Poland. And America welcomed her in 1898 with a statue that read: *Give me your tired, your poor, your huddled masses yearning to breathe free.* By the time she was 45 years old, she was a widow with six children under sixteen. And she could neither read nor speak English. Still the alternative, the Carpathian Mountains, had the scars of both world wars but here, she lived beyond life expectancy to age seventy-six. I couldn't speak her native language so never heard the story from *her* lips, only secondhand through her daughters. Though I was too young to appreciate the passion behind her story.

Only now with my own automatic washer and dryer do I think of that unyielding washboard and harsh cake of soap my grandmother used on washdays—to do laundry for eight people. I'm never held captive by the weather and never worry over a threatening rain that demands a rescue of clothesline matter. That outdoorsy smell of clothes dried in fresh air is nice but the time-consuming downside is surprise thunderstorms. If my grandmother had ever owned an iron, it would have been the flat style that had to be reheated atop the stove—requiring even more of her time. But even with the modern, electric iron that sprays and steams to abolish her old task of dampening the dry clothes, today I seldom use an iron, satisfied with the *permanent press* promise of the label.

Clothes dryers and new fabrics canceled the task of ironing in the sixties. And physical labor has nearly vanished now in first world countries. Tools have been with us since we came down from the trees over three million years ago. Even those early stone ones hastened evolution. Even mental labor is reduced today with the calculator that shrinks the need for basic, arithmetic skills, eliminating the need to memorize those boring multiplication tables. Electronic mail, texting and fax offer instant communication with one another. And grocery lists will be soon be generated by automated inventories, shifting it all to the World Wide Web for fulfillment. With little intervention. Without leaving home, I can now shop by sliding my fingers over a keyboard that quickly displays sale items. Postage and recently state tax are small issue for online shoppers. Sitting at home in front of the computer is easier than fighting crowds—fighting for parking spots. Resources through the myriad of computer programs and apps will only increase my future efficiency. Even the simplest of word processors reduces the time needed to search dictionary and thesaurus. And I can multi-task by talking on a cell phone while engaged in other activities— an example of the old adage of two *birds with one stone.*

Modern tools offer the gift of *time.* Leaving me with a gnawing question. What will I *do* with this stockpile of hours? Convenience is comforting, but is this the only goal of technology?

It's unlikely that even a portion of spare hours will go towards any previous pursuits. Old pursuits such as letter writing. Once a source of entertainment for both writer and receiver, as well as a dividend for historians, letter writing faltered with the invention of the telephone over a hundred years ago. Lingering through the forties as the Hallmark greeting card gained popularity, personal letters were finally buried by electronic mail. Now electronic mail has been outdated by the even faster action of texting. Because texting proved faster— more convenient.

It doesn't look as though those extra hours will be spent on sharpening culinary skills either. No longer restricted to Chinese and pizza takeouts of the past, I can buy fancy vacuum-packed meals and zap them at home. The original frozen dinners of the seventies eliminated hours of preparation time but were designed as single servings. Poor substitutes for homemade vittles. But current prepared foods are gourmet meals— gourmet, *family* meals. No longer proxies, frozen dinners of the 21st century are the fastest growing items in grocery stores today.

Maybe new pastimes will develop and fill those optional moments of time. Health clubs, larger now in size and scope, are possibilities. Except statistics don't bear out their worthy purpose. Reports are that obesity in America is at an all time high and reportedly will grow to 43% of the population in the next ten years. In 2012, Americans were 33% percent fatter than forty years ago. Models, twenty percent thinner than they use to be, have a better track record here, though I doubt that their svelte bodies can be credited all to exercise. They probably eat a lot less than average folks.

Extra time might allow for more reading— an often renewed vow. Large scale bookstores exist, where I can browse the day away. But reading as a pastime is 20% lower in the general population than it was twenty years ago, and public libraries, except for computer use, are in decline, as is the publishing world. Electronic books have increased in popularity, and their novelty will fill some of that extra time.

Time itself is elusive. Clichés tell the ambiguous story: *time waits for no man* and having too much *time on our hands* we *kill time*. All leading to the conclusion that time is coveted—in moderation. Homosapiens, relative to other species, are physically small but still around after three hundred thousand years. So I conclude that keeping track of time helped those ancestors. Those first timepieces, the sundials and hourglasses, supported their evolution. Quietly structuring their lives. Such timepieces were easy to ignore. While the modern ones offer all kinds of information— at a minimum, calendar dates and weather around the world—they're nosier than their predecessors and can't be ignored. Even wristwatches ring, buzz and flash. To attract our attention.

Attention. With all this spare time, we could become more attentive.

Attention seems a worthy consideration for those swells of time. Studies in child development show that given the choice between adult attention and a new toy, kids choose attention every time. Understanding the merits as do the young, mystics advise: *attend to each moment, smell the roses*—or anything else that the moment delivers. Take *one day at a time*. Neuroscientists put the advice another way. Studying how knowledge is acquired, they write: "Attention is almost magical in its ability to alter the brain." Giving attention to new skills can actually change brain structure? A rather big dividend.

Bits of attention account for little, like puzzle pieces scattered in a box holding no clue of the whole picture. In America, television ads interrupt programs at a minimum of every thirteen minutes to depict hurried, frustrated people who appear to foster the hope that the next moment will deliver what the previous one lacked. During a dull lecture, my attention wanders, and I may fall asleep. Something the speaker is less likely to do.

When I give my full attention over to an venture, I'm *lost* in it for awhile. Good or bad, I'm missing from the world and less critical of myself and others. The impression I make no longer counts. I stop judging others—a mutual gain in these moments. Teenage jargon offers insight too into a world where they remain observers; *get into it* teens instruct each other, a crafty demand to simply eliminate distractions. And then there are those spiritual possibilities for our attention. The goal of meditation calls for a clear mind, and the yoga stretches force followers to attend to their breathing. Seemingly rather mundane activities—that often leads to healthier bodies. Such focused attention appears to pay off in spades.

Words such as *focus* and *center* have seeped into the English lexicon over the last twenty years, suggesting a deepening of attention. In the forties, teachers demanded that kids "concentrate", directing them to filter out disparate thoughts. They asked kids to forget the possibilities for the newly falling snow visible from the school window as well as the kid in the next desk who insisted on aiming a variety of projectiles their way. Even then knowing that undivided attention carried a price, teachers ordered kids to pay attention.

Pay attention? There's a cost? Spare time carries the price tag of our priorities. We fill time with what seems important. Tools have shortened those tiresome tasks, but free hours fill without notice. And the magic of technology can't pickup the bill, or subsidize the cost. Attention means uninterrupted time devoted to—something. And those experiences, the ones that later tug at our spirits and leave us knowing that they were in the lofty category, require the time we *grant* them.

SIMON SAYS

I'm more relaxed knowing that voodoo dolls are no longer in circulation. Unlike modern terrorists, who usually take their own lives in the process of killing others, those old doers of black magic weren't near their subjects when they inflicted pain. In the comfort of their homes, these magicians inserted pins in rag dolls. The doll of course had to possess a *harmony* with the subject for the scheme to work. But playing on the superstitious nature of the populace in the Dark Ages, an era that ended about five hundred years ago, these magicians appear to have succeeded. The justice system lagged in those days so it's doubtful that the villains were ever punished for their evil deeds. Evidence was circumstantial at best. Though voodoo dolls disappeared, fear lingers from those times in the form of clowns and puppets. Why are such imposters so mysteriously scary for both kids and adults in the twenty-first century?

Like the old voodoo dolls, puppets and clowns are veiled, so I don't know how bad they are. Or could be. Current writers of horror novels present scary tales of such disguised entertainers who appear innocent but likely harbor evil intent. That puppeteer, whom I can't see pulling the strings, could be wicked. Like those magicians of the Dark Ages with their strange dolls and evil intentions. But maybe they were also onto a noteworthy human trait. Being evil doesn't eliminate the use of inborn gifts. My guess is that those voodoo masters were quite intuitive. And knew certain things, which didn't come through book reading.

I know certain things about my body without books or medical counsel. Even the world of twenty-first century medicine now considers this possibility. Though I appreciate my doctor's education, experience and expertise, I have a few insights about a body that I've lived with— for as long as I can remember. My time with the white coats can't all be spent on technical, medical answers recited *to* me. These days when I see my doctor for an annual check-up, I like that I'm questioned about my lifestyle. She seems interested in information *from* me, rather than repeating textbook data *to* me. I like that the word "patient" has been replaced with "client" in this relationship. Recent research suggests that invisible things such as m*y thoughts* and *feelings* affect my physical health. A quantum leap in medicine of the last twenty years.

I come by this doctor attitude naturally. Growing up, I never saw the generation who raised me going to doctors. They were so secure in taking care of themselves, none had health insurance: either hospital or physician. And in the end, that attitude paid off. No one ever got sick in that generation: neither my mother nor her four sisters. There was a family doctor who reassuringly stood in the wings for them, and everyone knew him by first name. But one went for a visit only on rare occasions: births, terminal illness or once a festering gardening thumb caused by an aberrant thorn. For common things like colds and flu, there were self-remedies. Things like annual check-ups were unheard of in this group.

Though not prematurely, two of my extended family died of untreated hypertension. Paying attention, I had high blood pressure on my radar a long time before medication was needed. I figured out the benefits of running for health twenty-five years before my doctor began to warn of family *tendencies*. I decided to act before medication was necessary. Not overweight but not particularly athletic, I began by running downhill, an extra house a day five days a week—rain, snow or shine. After two years I got my daily runs up to five miles. A force beyond that inherited doctor attitude overtook me. Wisdom was coming from the inside.

The inner wisdom of animals is taken for granted as part of their survival. In biology texts, it's known as instinct. Which in lower forms of life is natural and requires no learning period. Instincts insure the continuation of a species as when bees build hives, spiders: webs, birds: nests and ants colonies. Instincts force species to get necessary jobs done and can't be ignored. Or put to logic. Though angered by the insistent squirrel that digs holes in my groomed lawn to store nuts, carefully gathered for those winter days, I know that the cute rodent's instinct allows no choice.

Scientists claim that human instinct was shed during the process of evolution. Which grants me more freedom and places me at the top of the food chain—a significant gain. The evolutionists tell us that only remnants of the *fight or flight* instinct remain. My adrenaline energizes me when I feel endangered, and I can either stick around and fight or run. I just need to act. If on my running path I sight an ownerless, leash less dog bearing his teeth at me, I quickly reject the idea of a fight between us. My instinct is to run. The other way. Then my adult logic kicks in, and I know that an unchained dog is more likely to chase me if I run— so I *walk* away. Quite fast. Logic entails reflection while pure instinct is immediate. Those extended mental calculations proved costly for the cavemen, who were reportedly equipped with clubs. All of the time.

That lost human instinct evolved to what we now call *intuition*. Medical intuitive Caroline Myss defines the force of intuition as "*a primal sense that allows us to use energy data to make decisions in the immediate moment.*" Her definition widens instinct to include intelligence— maybe making intuition that elusive, sixth sense. But in the 21st century, the cultural attitude toward intuition is that it's rare— so most of us decline the title of psychic. The reality of such an innate skill is too fuzzy in this world of concrete things. So the accuracy of intuitive information remains doubtful. Things that appear *out of the blue* are classified as lowly "hunches." Unlike the insistent instinct so evident in lower species, intuition remains in the wings for us, lacking status. *I know this inside out: like the back of my hand; I'm going with my gut on this one* are phrases that imply intangible wisdom from the inside, not outside. And is likely what those voodoo magicians had.

The Dark Ages were replaced by The Enlightenment, which in turn ushered in a respect for items that could be *measured*, and birthed respected fields of physics, mathematics, astronomy and medicine. (Light and dark were used as metaphors for good and bad— until historians recognized the prejudice and renamed the Dark Ages the *Middle* Ages.) Hoping to extinguish the myths of the previous years of history, the Enlightenment accepted only objective reasoning and loosened the fears of the pervious era with rational thought —producing grand thinkers. Thinkers who rejected ideas that couldn't be supported with measurable facts.

Like all eras, the Enlightenment had its skeptics. The poet William Blake and the psychologist Karl Jung questioned whether everything *could* be measured—seemingly a fair question. Both men concluded that life contains a few intangibles, difficult to measure. Living during that Age of Enlightenment, but with a century between them, both Blake and Jung left classic bodies of work that until recently have been viewed as *too complex for the average* reader. Likely labeled "complex" because both man found fault with the enlightened era. Blake complained that the methods of the Enlightenment *"anesthetized"* the world and argued that only the inner wisdom of humans, intangible and immeasurable by all accounts, brought freshness to life. After his declaration, Blake continued to write of his mystical visions.

Karl Jung's theory of the collective unconscious leapt far beyond the definition of human intuition. He wrote that real power could be gained from the *collective* of human thought, that humans *shared* inner wisdom in this collective unconscious, which was outside awareness. Jung was trained as a medical doctor and wrote of our psychological heritage— our biological heritage had previously been documented by Charles Darwin. To his credit, he recognized from the beginning the subjective nature of his speculation.

Nor did Jung stop with the collective unconscious. He wrote that humans *caused* material items to manifest, making them the *source* of events rather than the powerless *recipients*. When a sufficient number of people hold the same idea, Jung claimed that it would appear in physical form. Though one inventor is assigned to each discovery, every creation belongs to the collective thoughts of many, he wrote.

When Jung's theory is applied to the automobile, Henry Ford still gets the credit. But simultaneously with Ford, many unnamed people had similar thoughts swirling around their minds. Jung writes that even those anonymous thoughts empowered Ford. Contemplating lands so distant, many unnamed humans knew that walking, horses, wagons and sailing would be impractical modes of future transport. Such a group eventually reaches a tipping point, (an actual number) and the concept spills into tangible expression through one person. Eventually one inventor emerges. But such an abstraction couldn't be measured in Jung's day. Or now.

Living today, Jung would likely smile at the present puzzle in physics over light that has haunted scientists: what determines the form natural light will take? Will it appear as a wave or a particle? Sounds simple but apparently is not. At the end of the 20th century, the field of quantum physics began to suggest that the power of human thought and feelings may have something to do with this old mystery. Could the form that light will take be influenced by the thoughts and feelings of the *researchers* who perform the experiments?

The Enlightenment sanitized the Dark Ages. And so thorough a cleaning ignored a bit of potential, leaving humans as powerless as those old voodoo dolls once did. But if I'm the source rather than recipient of an event, my perspective changes. Life isn't some enemy that must be tackled, as in the caution to "*face* life." I *am* life. Which grants me the inner wisdom of intuition and could change those old robot questions: will robots someday become human-like and replace me? Or will *I* become automated and more like them?

ATTENTION, PLEASE

I'm never bored with the legend of the sixth century king who created an experiment to appease his curiosity. With a desire to study language development, the ruler isolated five hundred newborns. Their physical needs would be met with as little human intervention as the times allowed. In an environment devoid of words, would the infants learn to talk, the creative king pondered. But the trial aborted itself, and he learned nothing of speech. None of the infants survived to the age that human speech appears. The tale's incidence in psychology texts convinces me of the truth of this early stab at research. Today, over a millennium after the event, textbooks attribute the infants' deaths to a lack of *tactile stimulation*. No one touched those babies. Mother cats forever licking their young know by instinct how to do the job right. A bit naive, that king meant well, but food and shelter weren't enough. Those fated infants of the sixth century needed something more.

It's unlikely that a control group existed in those distant days of the sixth century— so the result of the newborns being massaged by robots is unknown. All we know is that the five hundred infants got little human attention— through touch or any of the senses. And they all died before age two. Another study about the effects of surroundings on humans was done in Hawthorne, Illinois. This one conducted in 1970 was more scientific than the ancient king's. The governing board of a manufacturing plant in Hawthorne attempted to measure the importance of the environment on its workers. Would the workers' productivity be affected by different surroundings? Would efficiency increase? Questions that all good employers ask. Music was piped into the plant. Productivity increased. Music was stopped. Productivity increased. Paint was changed. Productivity increased. The original color was restored. And productivity increased. Regardless of the change, productivity increased. The researchers fought their way through the baffling results and concluded that it was not the *kind* of change that mattered, but the board's ongoing attention to its workers that increased output.

My grandmother often gave me attention by repeating a favorite story to anyone who would listen. Telling of a time I stood in the middle of her living room and managed to stand erect without help, of either furniture or an attending adult, I declared, "See this trick I can do!" She stressed in each retelling that I was eighteen months old when I made the proud assertion that I could stand alone. Explaining the punch line with a twinkle in her eye, she then announced that my great "trick" could have been achieved by a child half my age — but my speech was that of a child twice my age. I'm not sure why I chose to file her tale in my memory. Maybe it was her repetition that caused my psyche to label it important. Maybe it was because it was my *grand*mother. I only know that that slice of attention caused me to actually shape a personality around the tale. As a result, I've gotten more attention for my verbal skills than for the physical ones over the years.

With little conscious notice over the years, I've carefully filed those responses to me that supported her story. And allowed ones that denied it to fade. I marched in a corps of cadets, biked and ran over the years but those all fall under the exercise label, not athletics. I wasn't athletic. I'd decided on that long before when I chose my grandmother's story for an early beacon in my life. I translated attention from others through the lens of her story.

The fact that I remember the distant incident so clearly officially places it in Adlerian psychology's *earliest recollection* category. I probably remember her story and not the incident itself, but Adlerian psych finds this detail minor. Good or bad, I made a crucial decision in the choice of her story and used that thread to weave a personality— and by age six, like most of us, I had one. Certain traits distinguished me at six that couldn't have been said of me at eighteen months. My personality grew from attention— from those responses to me that I'd decided to keep. This isn't fate. All attention falls to the recipient to file or discard.

Kids seize *any* attention that they can get, especially from grownups, and detest being ignored: collecting *no* attention. As with adults, kids look for a response, sometimes choosing bad behavior over good, because bad behavior assures a reaction, usually from embarrassed parents. Good behavior, obeying the rules, is often taken for granted by innocent parents. Who fail to acknowledge it.

Attention to emotional development began to catch up to physical development midway through the twentieth century. Previous research into that first year of life gave little notice of the emotional side of life. Ages that babies rolled over, sat, stood and finally walked were well documented. Thirty years ago, a smile from a baby less than three months was *due to gas* and not to be mistaken for joy. A smile didn't mean that a baby was happy in your presence. The attitude was that newborns had little, if any, interaction with their environment. Now psychologists are looking at infants' *feelings* in those first three months. We've learned that a *fetus* knows the mother's voice by the second trimester of *pregnancy.* Before birth. Words such as bonding: attachment and detachment with the biological mother abound. Psychologists now agree that newborns register their surroundings. And doctors have appropriately adjusted delivery room actions. The classic slap on the baby's rear and circumcision are hardly welcoming actions. In the first three months, infants do register the smiles, coos and pheromones of their caregivers. Nature plans that well. Most of us respond to babies with a smile. We expect nothing from them. Babies of any kind never feel like strangers to us.

But attention to strangers over age eight is narrowed by perceptions. Though not always successful, I try and tread carefully in the area of stereotypes—searching for a positive side to those who are dimly cast. Senior citizens offer much in the form of mentorship to all ages, but their need of physical help often determines my response. Teens' unmatched energy and idealism suggest the possibility of a better world when not overshadowed by their publicized problems. And then there are broad generalities that shape attention: males are self-reliant and women are dependent. When a woman driver takes out a map, an offer of help arises—with the assumption that she's lost. While the likely conclusion around a man sitting with map in-hand on the side of the road is that he's exploring new territory. Hardly in need of aid.

Attention comes *to* us and what we do with it is up to us.

The gay, bisexual, lesbian and transgender, the GBLT folks, have chosen to accept negative attention. By giving it a positive slant. Reference to themselves as "queer", an old word, is now acceptable because *queer* also means remarkable. The gay community, with a sexual orientation out of the mainstream, has bravely taken steps into uncharted territory.

I started to give real attention to others during the encounter movement of the seventies. When sensitivity training reigned. At first the coincidence of interesting people, who always seemed to comprise my groups, surprised me. Until I realized that this wasn't Lady Luck in my corner. I devoted time to these group experiences so they were more intense than even my close friendships. By attending to the stories of others, I found myself surrounded by engaging people. I was forced to experience the moment which nicely stopped my mind from jumping back and forth into tomorrow and yesterday.

And then there's attention to other forms of life. The benefits of talking to plants and touching pets are well documented. And dentists tell us that the mere act of flossing teeth can extend human lives by nearly two years. Even my teeth benefit from notice.

But these days, the majority of human attention is on one screen or another. When I'm in a crowd, I often turn, thinking that someone is speaking to me, aware of me, only to find them— on an I-phone, totally unaware of my existence. Technology delivers the gadgets and then the screens fill with all kinds of interesting images that change with the touch of a finger. Leaving human attention, that one-to-one kind, pretty sparse. Facebook offers convenience and contacts—though the latter is from such a distance that charlatans paint all sorts of images. But not all are fakes. Millions put pieces of their lives on this popular social network, defining themselves through screen images. In his book *Talking Back to Facebook,* author James Steyer writes, *the young present themselves before they introspect.* These are not people trying to trick anyone Steyer concludes; they simply don't know themselves well enough for such public proclamations.

In the eighties, a study was done in a variety of American libraries. The focus was attention through touch and its significance to the library visitor. (Eye contact and words were variables not constants in this research.) During the visits, library attendants purposely, but casually, touched the hands of some of the participants when checking out books— while not touching others. Simple actions. But when participants were interviewed immediately after visiting each of the targeted libraries, again and again those whose hands had been lightly touched spoke of the library as: "friendly, well-stocked, orderly, quiet." A big difference in these public libraries was reported, and the reason was the mere touch of a hand. There's power behind our attention, our responses to each other, and even the casual ones count. Social networking has its place but fails the tactile test —just as did the methods of the ancient king. Those fated infants got no response from the world.

STRONG MEDICINE

I propose a second look at the placebo effect. When sugar pills produce recoveries, heads ought to turn. Such marvels deserve immediate notice. Participants in medical studies sometimes heal from a placebo, substances that have *no known effect* on bodies. Believing that a potent drug is at work and ignorant of the nature of their drug, they heal from — a sugar pill. Such healing, known as the placebo effect, is an attractive prospect. These inert pills cost nearly nothing in dollars and cents, nor do they meddle in body functions. When placebos heal, bodies respond to mental instructions. The only glitch is that the phenomenon works when participants are kept in the dark. They can't know the truth: that the pill has no active ingredient. Even physicians aren't in agreement on the event. Such a phenomenon deserves reflection.

The placebo effect in medicine is a little like the old power of suggestion. When I hear of a prison break on the news, I get goose bumps at every creak in my house, especially at a late hour. Warnings and re-calls of foods, whether or not I've eaten the troubled brand, make my stomach churn. Reports of icy roads within fifty miles of a planned trip turn me into a fearful driver. Still, the placebo effect is bigger than my paranoia. Placebo does more than produce a feeling. The mind sends a message, and the physical body changes. The body heals. But the happening is forever qualified with the word *only;* it's *only* the placebo effect. Implying its worthlessness. Though the mind healing the body seems noteworthy to me.

In my twenties, I first got sick with what the doctors then diagnosed as "colitis." Over the years, colitis in medical journals has morphed to spastic colon and then Irritable Bowel Syndrome. The last, now with its own acronym, IBS, will no doubt endure. With IBS, a body doesn't digest food in the right way—and prematurely loses nutrients. During my bouts with the disorder over the years, I lose weight and am forced to break routines. One doesn't wander far from the familiar with this infirmity.

Later as a single mom with two teenagers and a demanding job that included more teenagers, I grasped the obvious. Putting two and two together— I saw that IBS came on me when life was stressful. My body sensed the stress and responded with a *helpful* disorder. The IBS kept me home, and safe and secure I managed to get my emotions together. The periods proved useful time-outs, and once the stress lifted, the symptoms quickly vanished. Without need of medication. Sometimes, my doctor prescribed a sedative that simply put me to sleep, and the trauma lifted. IBS isn't traceable to germs or eating habits. Or even genes. It could be argued that I *inherited* a weak colon— or maybe never learned to deal with high levels of stress. But the two, the IBS and the stress, forever arriving in harmony is beyond coincidence.

Research supports this connection between mind and body—my body's response to my thoughts.

Those intangible feelings and the tangible body collide all the time, in my case stress and colon. Fear can raise heartbeats and blood pressure, bringing about a tightening of intestines. Fear also energizes with the hormone adrenaline, just in case the need to run arises— in case there's a need for a quick getaway. The feeling of sadness is usually accompanied by a lack of energy while anger has a stimulating effect. Satisfying meals are shown more nutritious than those gulped ones; in fact the body hardly seems to note the nutrients of the latter. After extensive exercise, brains release chemicals known as endorphins that carry feelings of well-being. And of course sexual feelings deliver physical changes consistent with the task at hand.

Technology offers a process known as biofeedback. Mechanical monitors are connected to a body, and data is fed back to the conscious person in hopes of understanding this complicated mind/body relationship. Unlike that positive placebo effect, some interactions between mind and body are onerous to owners. Hypertension, eczema, asthma, rheumatoid arthritis and migraines carry the generic name of psychosomatic—literally mind *directing* body. Sometimes painfully. Such ailments are defined by the American Medical Association as ones with *physical symptoms but no known, external cause.* The definition suggests that such ailments are controlled by feelings. And perhaps even originate in the mind. Hoping to explain the situation in tangible ways, modern medicine looks for concrete causes for these puzzling ailments. The origins of hypertension could be: too much salt in the diet, obesity, excessive alcohol consumption and lack of exercise. Or a combination of all these factors. But when all deductions have been eliminated, only heredity remains—and is tagged the culprit.

Psychosomatic illnesses have had additions and deletions over the years. Making an official list tentative at any given moment. A modern index would likely include the malady known as anorexia, an ailment whose symptoms are painfully obvious; the patient continually loses appetite and thus weight and becomes skeletal in appearance. When the illness is tied to the state known as bulimia, it's worsened with laxatives and induced vomiting to guarantee weight loss. Refusing to admit their declining health, even viewing their ghostly images in mirrors, victims of anorexia/bulimia literally starve to death. Unless a dramatic intervention occurs. Even after its thirty year scourge on American culture, it can't be proven that victims have actually caught a germ or virus. Or even inherited a frightful gene. Only profiles exist as to the *personality* and *gender* that is likely to acquire this eating disorder.

A hundred years ago, Sigmund Freud studied a similar condition known as hysteria. Like anorexia, hysteria had physical symptoms but no known cause. Freud, the *father of psychology* and also a medical doctor, concluded that the trauma of World War I brought on hysteria. Settling into the collective human mind, the ordeal of war caused victims to become physically paralyzed, he wrote. Freud's deduction implied that hysteria had roots in the mind, which carried the cultural values of his day. Today hysteria falls under the umbrella of mental illness because it's no longer accompanied by physical symptoms. If the trauma of war can settle into minds and paralyze bodies, then an ailment such as anorexia/bulimia is likely linked to the cultural value of thin—especially in 21st century America where *thin* means a size 0 and ribs show.

I don't know their eating habits, but models and movie stars have become thinner over the last fifty years. Models who want to walk the runway must have *at least* an 18.5 BMI (body mass index). Fifty years ago this number was 20—making the models then a bit heavier. Things seemed to have reversed themselves; in the past it was difficult to get *down* to 20, but today models have trouble getting *up* to 18.5. Some models in 21st century America are so skeletal that audiences are repulsed, not an effective way to sell clothes Not surprising, the sufferers of anorexia/bulimia are mostly female. The victims have *caught* a culture—that emphasizes a very thin female.

Mind and body are obviously in a collusion of sorts, but its nature remains elusive. Pregnancies of mothers under stress end in the births of unhealthy babies. This is a fact. A pregnant mother's emotions affect *both* bodies. Statistically beyond coincidence are terminal patients of any disease who often live a bit longer in order to celebrate anniversaries or the arrival of loved ones. Their willpower seems to postpone death. And those cancer survivors, who *debate* with their oncologists about treatment, also survive beyond coincidence. Cancer has one medical diagnosis: callous cells multiply uncontrollably and destroy the healthy ones. But the disease is defined differently by those who experience it. As in most matters, individuality peeks through. And even in this deadly illness of cancer, none fall sick in standard ways. Actually there is no standard way to be sick. Living in close proximity to one another on the same planet, we're all exposed to similar "bugs" but fall sick and encounter illness, even the same *one*, in different ways. Even that final declaration of "I'm sick" varies among us—some choose bed rest for the flu, while others do their best to ignore it.

Only the common verbs of illness are similar. When I'm sick, I've *caught* something. Learned from the culture, I must now *fight* those *enemies* within: virus, bacteria, and germs are fought with pills— those tangible, expensive items that have become sacred *artillery*. But these warlike verbs of fighting and artillery aren't necessary when bodies heal naturally—from burns, abrasions, extracted teeth and blisters. Still for the big jobs around disease, the big guns of antibiotics and steroids are pulled out.

Andrew Weil, the popular guru of alternative medicine today, writes: *Because of the material orientation of the society, a failure to accept anything without a material base exists. External, material objects (virus, bacteria, parasites) never cause disease. Whether or not the individual is susceptible is the determinant.* Let's not lose track of that little sugar pill that often brings on the mysterious placebo. When this happens, the sugar pill prompts a mental trick that triggers an inside power. A power that is so difficult to claim that a tangible pill is required to do the job. But if psychosomatic illnesses are *all in our heads* as the definition implies, the cure likely lies there too.

THE CONTRARY SENTINEL

I've never been under hypnosis. There's something about the preposition *under* that scares me. Under the gun: Under the weather: Under the knife: Under investigation: Underground: Put under. None are endearing. When I think of hypnosis, *under* gets in the way from the start. A trance, controlled by someone whose motives are vague, threatens my survival instincts. The experts suggest that 60% of the population is difficult to hypnotize, and my reluctance may make me one of these holdouts. Though I admit that I'm fascinated by such a process. Centuries old, hypnosis has succeeded in reducing the pains of childbirth and dentistry, even defeating bad habits such as overeating and cigarette smoking. Even those experiencing pain in lost limbs, known as phantom limbs, have been helped by the process. But the slapstick of stage hypnosis stunts its promise. When an audience is entertained by the antics of a subject under another's control, the practice remains on the fringes of medicine. Such power surely has a better use?

Hypnosis by definition is a *sleep-like* state. Night sleep, also another state of consciousness, is better known but lacks the trance-like awareness of hypnosis. As far as I can tell the closest I've ever been to the hypnotic state is when I was lead into meditation— by an expert guru. I didn't check the guru's credentials beforehand but doubt there's licensing in this line of work. I had only a name, a location— and approval by an author. An author renowned for writing books but not meditative states. I was at a *why not* stage of my life. Though the country was not. It was 1985 and the Mondale/Ferraro ticket had been defeated by a landside the previous year by the sitting president, Ronald Reagan. Unlike me, the country wasn't in an experimental mood: a *woman* on the ticket of a major party? a woman one step away from the most powerful position on earth? The Woman's Movement had just seen the Equal Rights Amendment (the ERA) go down. So the *word on the streets* remained: women were too emotional for such authority, too often sidetracked by pregnancy—that insistent mothering instinct. Status Quo in America reigned in 1985.

But maintaining my spirit of adventure, I flew to New York City in the fall of that year for a two day meditation workshop with a real guru. She first taught a group of about hundred people how to properly sit on the floor with a minimum of back support. Then added a mantra accompanied by relaxing music. The guru's voice lead the way, just as I'm sure a seasoned hypnotist does. There were breaks with light food and light talk from other presenters. Then the group returned to the serious business of meditation, and the meditative state increased until one session lasted an hour. Though I had done nothing more than sit cross-legged on the floor silently repeating a mantra —for a total of 10 hours over two days—physically and emotionally, I felt great for weeks after the experience. For weeks I felt peaceful and *light*. Different than I had ever felt before, though I'd had less social interaction, exercise and fresh air, during that weekend. I hadn't done the professed, healthy things. The meditation left me wondering exactly what had happened. What had *I* done? Meditation jargon would dictate that I'd simply cleared my mind. This was the extent of my input in the process? That would seem about the same input I have in my immune system.

The medical world has seen that there are no stage attics in the field of immunology—so the field gets Federal research money. My immune system resists ailments by distinguishing my body from others. The system seems to know who's who. Possessing fierce rejection mechanisms that are used unmercifully on perceived intruders; my immunities serve as gatekeepers of my physical health. And provide unmatched security even in this postmodern age.

I know that my immune system is made up of groups of cells, molecules, and organs. Workers, certain large white blood cells, wander through my body consuming foreign particles such as dust, asbestos, and bacteria. Without my conscious direction. The shrewd system makes decisions about what stays and what goes— and even flaunts memory. Recalling that an invader has paid a previous visit, immunities prepare a stronger defense. Producing antibodies, immunities are strengthened with a second exposure to an illness. So childhood diseases are only suffered once. These efficient sentries are nature's first concern. For twenty-four hours before milk begins to flow from human mothers, a newborn receives a substance from the breast which acts as an immunizing agent, while the baby's own are gearing up for future action. Immunities destroy aliens that could spread disease, hindering their entrance through such gates as tears, mucus, and saliva. Sneezing, fever and rapid inflammation are protective measures— red flares from the immune system to get our attention in what might be a serious matter.

Three big ailments in America: AIDS, cancer, and allergies all have roots in immunities. AIDS has an identified virus (HIV) that causes the immune system to dysfunction and finally shut down altogether, making the owner susceptible to any disease. No virus has been identified with cancer, but the immune system fails at its job here—and accepts aliens. Researchers aren't in agreement as to why the system fails to reject the growth of abnormal cancer cells. Even more puzzlingly is the fact that in lower forms of life without immune systems, cancer is nonexistent— suggesting a mysterious link between immunities and this dreaded disease of cancer. With allergies, the immune system becomes *choosy* and overreacts with common foods and ordinary life encounters such as bee stings and house dust. Labeling these common items *villains* by producing hives, sneezing, and labored breathing, the immune system shows little mercy here. Allergic reactions have been known to cause death. But once the troublemaker is identified, allergies are the easiest of three to control.

Though an ally, the immune system can be frustrating. Medicine has learned to transplant new organs into bodies—often a life-saving process. Immunities rightfully identify the new organ as a poacher. And doctors are then forced to fight the system's rejection mechanism by *lowering* immunities— a risky act because the body then becomes vulnerable. With the disease known as pulmonary fibrosis, immunities fill the smokers' lungs with fibers as *protection* from the toxins of cigarette smoke. Though maddening, their labor is still clear. These sentinels are still working in our behalf.

Immunities are there to protect us. Except on those occasions when they kill us.

Rational questions arise when the immune system reacts to normal parts of bodies by producing *destructive* antibodies. Diseases now labeled *auto*immune: Multiple Sclerosis, Type I Diabetes, Crones, Rheumatic Fever, and Lupus are a result of such reactions. (Lupus is on the rise today.) In these cases the immune system seems to have lost track in the identity of the body that it's protecting. Things run amuck, and the conclusion is often death rather than deliverance. Hoping to outfox the immunities in some of these puzzling cases, medicine has brought us new drugs. By ingesting these BRMs, *biological response modifiers*, patients can lower the immune response this time by blocking communication between the system's workers. Still, this attempt to control the system through a roadblock seems tentative at best to me. In most endeavors, cooperation has a better success rate than blockades. Immunities are also lowered naturally by stress; since stress provides quick energy to the body and releases hormones such as adrenaline—it inhibits the immune system. But foiling a system that usually works in our behalf may not be the best solution either.

Maybe modern life has confused immune systems. Echkart Tolle, a spiritual leader not aligned with any particular religion, offers a suggestion. He proposes that attention to our *inner* body strengthens the immune system. Warning that most attention these days is on the *outer* body in the form of appearance: clothes: weight: plastic surgery—thus neglecting *inner* body needs. Tolle suggests that we set a regular time aside to *feel* what's within. Conjuring a view of such things as heart, bones and muscle, which quickly brings on a sudden tingling in hands and feet, indicating a response from the body. Tolle counsels that by focusing on the breath, as it enters and exits, the abdomens will follow the rhythm. And finally bodies will be flooded with energy: similar to the effects of yoga and meditation.

Awareness of sensory experience, rather than the outside world, circles us back to hypnosis. Centering on the five senses and the voice of that hypnotist, subjects under hypnosis are open to suggestion. Told by the hypnotist that an allergen has touched them, subjects display skin reactions. Sensory changes have been recorded when those in the hypnotic state have smelling salts defined as a "delightful perfume" and fail to reject the repelling odor. During deep hypnosis, awareness appears so broad that subjects lose a sense of identity—who they are. Even such things as written signatures change. And warts have been known to disappear when so instructed by the hypnotist. Warts, those inert appendages so obviously *not* us, are tolerated by our immune system; no rejection reaction occurs to signal their illegal appearance. But hypnotized people *do* recognize warts as aliens. A positive sign.

Both hypnosis and the immune system have guides. And with those deadly autoimmune diseases looming, it's time to step up and claim that position. Taking the hypnotist's job, we could learn to self-hypnotize. And with Tolle's simple advice, lead ourselves to the power of our own inner voice. With this new power, it will be clearer to that enigmatic, immune system exactly who we are. Spontaneous remission of disease does occur. As some have found that imposing voice.

NOT A SPECTATOR SPORT

I'm cautious of my facts these days. With confidence that information so labeled would remain true forever, I memorized lots of facts in school. Once something is declared a *fact*, shouldn't the chance of change be slim? Maybe over centuries revelations by science alters matters, as when the age-old belief that the earth was flat proved phony. But when information appears and then changes in less than a decade, I don doubt. What could be more factual than the Government's official food pyramid that appeared in the early nineties? An easy image that offered information on how to stay healthy, the pyramid was issued by the USDA (United States Dept of Agriculture) with advice from the NSA (National Science Association) to comply with the FDA (Food & Drug Administration.) Such agencies carry clout. This thumbnail sketch provided by the pyramid was hardly a whim. But a decade after its debut, the pyramid has vanished—certain *truths* proved faulty. When are facts certain? Do we need another category, somewhere between *yes* and *no?*

Ten years of ingesting less fat, as the pyramid promoted, a startling statistic on obesity appeared. One third of the American population is obese. And another thirty percent is overweight. In 2013, half the American population is simply fat. As both the obese and overweight groups include children, red flags are waving—rather wildly. Once appearing as a convenient, frig magnet, the original food pyramid is no where to be found today. If heads didn't roll in the government agencies that developed the handy pyramid, red faces surely float in the wake of its demise.

Fat free became the advertisers' guarantee of success on all food products in the nineties. Cholesterol became the villain. There's a logic to *fat makes you fat* that slips right into the cultural attitude toward thin bodies in America. But not all fat is the same, and I sensed doubt in nutritional circles when the phrase "good cholesterol" surfaced. Some fat is needed in healthy diets, and even in my limited knowledge of nutrition, I know that protein is needed to *burn* fat and strengthen arteries. But in the crusade to eliminate all fat in the nineties, protein was replaced with *fat free carbs*: white sugar. But carbohydrates create cravings for more sugar so a cycle was created that likely accounts for the present obesity in America. The goal now is to watch the *kind* of fat, making sure to have sufficient protein in the mix. In the fat versus carbs controversy over health, white sugar has replaced fat as the new villain. Now in the millennium, there are good and bad sugars.

A young mother in the sixties, I followed a family message that breast-fed babies were healthier. Like most new mothers, I was determined to do the right thing and followed the family dictum to nurse my babies—though such advice ran counter to the cultural message. Breast feeding had begun its downward slide in cultural value as Playtex bottles, and their convenient, disposable liners, appeared in the late fifties; the new design promised convenience as well as less air intake than previous glass bottles. Since women were just beginning to hope for a place of equity in the professional workplace, the market timing for Playtex was perfect. Nursing a baby, especially in public, wasn't politically correct then. It didn't fit the profile of the working woman, just freed by Betty Freidan. The cultural perception of the wet nurse as lower class made the time right for bottle-fed babies. Now, fifty years later with a woman's place in the workplace firmly set, the benefits of breast feeding are off the charts.

I also laid my infants on their stomachs in the crib. Then it was a fact that babies on their stomachs were safer than those sleeping on their backs. If the newly functioning digestive system caused them to spit up, they wouldn't choke to death because the sour milk would simply fall from their mouths—which isn't the case when lying on their backs. That was the story then, but now in the millennium, unexplained crib deaths have entered the conversation. Quickly given the acronym SIDS (Sudden Infant Death Syndrome), such deaths have been blamed on weak neck muscles. The fear of infants choking to death has been replaced by the fear of them suffocating.

Many facts are directed by cultural attitudes as well as research.

Working in a public school in 1975, I found myself muddling through a fact change in American education. The Federal Dept of Education, through Special Education, mandated public schools to recognize and test for *Learning* Disabilities. Those kids so labeled would be given special services. Previously, physically disabled kids had been identified, and special accommodations had been made for left-handed students and reading problems caused by a disorder called dyslexia, defined as the reversal of letters and a lack of a left to right orientation. Now including emotionally disabled kids, the new law was broader. And would continue to expand.

Pushing for more welcoming, less rigorous, schools, attitudes had changed. Parents soon demanded more than quarterly report cards from schools. Weekly progress reports were requested—and delivered to parents by *the school*. Parents, fearful of alienating their children, defended them to teachers, while the main players, the kids, were eliminated from the loop. Had new facts about learning arisen in the seventies to bring on such changes? Or had attitudes about kids changed? In the late sixties, throngs of flower *children* had left home for California to follow the tone of the times— instead of their parents. And a solution to end the dramatic exodus began in public schools.

By the eighties, Leaning Disabilities included the three A's: ADHD, ADD and Autism. Without acronyms, known as hyperactivity, attention deficit disorder and the then little known neurological disorder called autism. All joined the ranks of the burgeoning category of potential learning disabilities in school kids. Autism, the most puzzling, was defined as *flawed, emotional development*. It seems that interpretation of the world, as defined, was difficult if not impossible for these kids. By 1985, the Diagnostic and Statistical Manual of Mental Disorders officially listed the three, big A's—making kids so labeled learning disabled and eligible for Special Services in public schools. New *facts* were born. Anthropologist Roy Gringer writes that the number of children diagnosed as autistic has increased by 130 percent from 1994 to 2006. (And continues to rise.) He attributes such a rise, in a mere twelve years, to "shifting definitions and cultural changes that affect perception and how scientists do their work."

Cultural attitudes alter facts and how scientists do their work?

Just as that migration of the young to California in the sixties changed facts about education, 911 changed the mindset of the nineties. The economy and stock market soared in America before the 911 tragedy. More millionaires were made in the nineties than ever before in American history. Bombarded with a rash of books and TV shows about money, middle class citizens talked in a new way about becoming rich. Then religious extremists made their presence known throughout the world by destroying both themselves and thousands of Americans religion replaced money in import. A born-again Christian served two terms as the President of the United States, and bookstores replaced books on money with entire sections devoted to inspirational books written by Fundamentalist Christians. The new tone downgraded Charles Darwin's previous work on evolution from fact to *theory*— though previously the majority of scientists had come to consensus on Darwin's work as fact.

The mindset of America in the twenty-first century honors thin and young. Old is out and young is in. Young and thin, especially in women, lie in the zone of perfection. While old and fat are in the *anything but* region. Fashion models and movie stars abide in this zone of perfection; what is fashion if not a cultural attitude? Youth and vitality are aligned with estrogen in females. But nature decreases the production of estrogen in the female body around age fifty, eliminating the possibility of pregnancy. So the necessity for estrogen replacement became a fact— until 2004 when such replacement began to show adverse effects in post menopausal women. After thirty years of following medical advice to ingest estrogen, before, during and after menopause, American women found that such action didn't extend lives as previously reported. Though eliminating some of the bothers of the Change such as hot flashes and mood swings, estrogen increased chances of an untimely death from heart trouble and breast cancer. And women discovered that the youthful appearance they hoped to retain with its replacement instead gave way to an early death. Appearing young in a casket has few perks.

The mindset of the times shoulders lots of names and is a force potent enough to have affected biology. Somewhere in the process of human evolution, females became preeners, while in other species, males are the colorful ones of the duo; the elaborate tail feathers of the peacock shadows that drab peahen. Except for humans, it's the male of the species who competes for the right to mate, while females appear indifferent to the outcome — relying on nature to determine the best father for her young. But such an arrangement can't work in the paternal culture humans have created. How can males be in charge while busily preening? Attitudes change even such mating matters.

In the days of the Greek and Roman Empires, women were classified as sexy if they dwelt on the *plump* side. The eating disorder known today as anorexia (extreme thinness through unhealthy diet) was unknown in these days, but had it existed then, its extreme would have been *gluttony*. Attitudes taken to the extreme— too fat or too thin—lead to calamity. Best a hold be placed on some of those items labeled *facts* today. And new information in the future carry *probability* labels, raising the word *maybe* to a new status. The nature of our cultural attitudes create uncertainty around "facts." The job doesn't lie solely with the scientist. It's a participatory world. We're all involved.

THE THREE R'S REVISITED

I'm averse to being cloned. Though I offer a rational defense on the subject, my ego is bruised by this declaration. But aside from my personal penchants, the wonders of living in the dawn of such discoveries as cloning, DNA and the human genome, haven't escaped me. Biologists now know that each human cell has thirty thousand genes—and that chimps, a species of monkey, possess only three hundred less. Again fueled by my ego, I reason that those three hundred genes that separate me from the chimp, a mere one percent of the total, made quite a difference in evolution. Scientists have yet to identify the function of each gene so the story remains unfinished. Even as mysteries are solved, others replace them. Maybe we need more thinkers: a greater variety.

Once I thought that science would eventually explain everything about both life and the universe. Smugly, I was sure that it would happen in my lifetime. But the notion evolved from my ignorance of scientific remnants those unanswered leftovers of pervious theories. Even in this post modern era of the twenty-first century, there remain questions—gnawing ones, usually unheard of by lay people like me. Why has the sturdy dinosaur, along with 90% of *all* species, become extinct? Some claim that dinosaurs didn't become extinct but rather that they evolved into birds: cute tiny birds? Still baffling. Why do viruses, unable to carry out their own reproduction like the rest of us, force the job onto their hosts? How did such a fragile organ as the eye evolve in so many different species? How does sap defy gravity by rising in the trees each year? How can the theory that the universe is infinite ever be confirmed?

An answer to the last question was attempted by a German astronomer born in the eighteenth century. Olbers theorized that the night sky would be evenly illuminated with stars in every direction if the universe were infinite. Of course his reasoning means that there would be no night—a problem right from the start. Contradictions don't set well with scientists so eventually Olbers was challenged by another astronomer who showed that the sky was dark at night because distant stars couldn't be seen. But his theory depends on the universe having a finite size—which can't be proven either. Though not well publicized, such research is well-recorded in the fields of science and math. Though still puzzling, remnants in the field are clear.

In less exacting fields, where *humans* are factors—things get foggy.

Social institutions such as public schools tussle with lots of mysteries. Compared to today, the school rules in America that *sought* to solve problems of the forties now border on the absurd. One worry then was students *obeying* teachers. In 2013, the fear is that kids will bring weapons to school and *shoot* teachers. A rule of the forties, which banned chewing *gum* in class, has morphed to warnings about swallowing *drugs* in school. A rule of the forties forbade kids from wearing *improper* clothing to school. But this rule was abolished in the seventies with the elimination of dress codes for both kids and teachers—female teachers could wear slacks to work. More important than what kids *wear* to school in the twenty-century is youth *suicide*.

As an educator my greatest mystery is less abstract. Mine is personal. Why did the best student I ever had take his life—when he was nineteen years old? Finishing his first year of college at full scholarship, Russ chose to cut short his time on earth. Though isolation is forever cited as the cause of youth suicide, I wouldn't have labeled him unpopular with his peers. But popular doesn't fit either. The gentler term "loner" fit Russ. His peers likely called him a "nerd." Failing to fit into their world of high school popularity with a *cool* attitude, Russ can't be pigeonholed. His peers liked him but didn't know where to place him. He followed school rules and made excellent grades. He wasn't a bad guy: a discipline problem or a truant. He was always present, never missing school or social conversation. His love of learning took him nightly at age sixteen to the local library, a place where his peers failed to frequent. Most of them didn't know its location. Russ studied to satisfy his own hunger while his peers involved themselves in sports— and each other. He may not have seen it as I did, but his peers were secretly in awe of him.

Russ chose not to do any of the big extras in high school: music, sports: drama. Music and sports carry a price tag for parents, money that Russ' parents didn't have. He had a girlfriend for a while, but at least at the time, a love relationship wasn't his thing either. Though good looking, smart and curious, a Romeo he was not, at least not during those high school years. And he failed to find a niche for himself even in advanced education. But not all nerds are suicides. Some, like the American computer giants of the century, Bill Gates, Steve Jobs and Mark Zuckleberg, manage to navigate through the tough terrain. Until they find a comfortable slot. The most useful thing I could have offered Russ was an assurance that *his* place at the table was significant. That we needed him. Life needed him.

Conformity in public schools today simplifies administration—for principals, teachers and staff. And revolves around popular students. *Popular* students are so labeled for the first time by their peers in middle school, just as puberty begins to set-in. And their self-consciousness becomes visible. In the middle and high school years, these popular kids conform and manage to abide by the rules of both the school and their peers. Usually making good grades, such kids are involved in school activities: sports, music, drama. All are well-liked by teachers and coaches. Though not a negative model by itself, these stereotypes offer the popular ones an exclusive position— and create outsiders. Outsiders, the *different* ones, like Russ, who don't pigeonhole well.

Differences among kids in public schools forever challenge educators. Should classes be homogeneous—college prep: general? Or heterogeneous, without consideration for levels of skill and future plans? And then there's the category of Learning Disabilities. Identified with such a deficit, Russ might have been spotlighted, but he had none. He just liked to read and learn. He might have found a niche had he known about those mysteries of science, but I doubt that even a bright kid like Russ knew about the remnants.

Adults are in charge and make the rules so kids assume that the job is done, that they have time for other pursuits. Sadly, lots of those under nineteen, still in high school in America today aren't interested in anything more mysterious than new apps for their I-phones— and bizarre clothes. As untied sneakers receive instant correction by adults, those flying shoestrings are either a plea for attention or an unconscious protest to Velcro. Pants that reveal belly buttons are popular but tricky today. To display belly buttons, jeans must be a number of inches below the feet so that the hems soon become frayed from being tread upon. Fortunately at this age, balance is near perfect. Bright colors of purple, red and blue are popular hair dyes that rub into pillows throughout homes. And the care of multiple body punctures burns most of their additional free time. Time might be spent on those long-standing mysteries and even their doubts and questions would help. Because adults don't have it all figured out.

The focus of the last fifteen years in America has been technology: tools of entertainment and convenience. Not the growing ill health of planet earth—threatened planet earth. Only young minds with new perspectives can shape that promised *fresh future*. Because their input's vital, youth needs to hear the questions. The personal computer's invention, though in homes since the nineties, began in the forties by those *under* forty. Seymour Cary at age 26 helped to replace vacuum tubes with transistors; Jack Kilby at age 35 founded the integrated circuit and Howard Aiken at age 37 came up with the first programmable computer. Finally followed by Steve Jobs who at age 30 pulled a persona computer together: the Apple I.

Though computers weren't around four thousand years ago, Ancient Greece got the question right. A long time ago, the Greeks knew that diverse thinking was important and defined "educate" *as the promotion of innate talents*. Rather than the teaching of accepted patterns, as American schools do today, they concluded that the starting point of education was to *draw out* what was innately *within* kids—and nurture it. In this ancient civilization, what adults could *impart* to the young was not the priority. Those Ancient Greeks wanted new stuff.

Diverse thinking is needed for invention as well as those riddles that neither scientist nor educator have so far solved. Differences are honored by Mother Nature so She does little cloning Herself. The closest Nature comes to duplication is identical twins, and these appear only once in every 350 births. (The multiple births of the last twenty years are the result of human work done in fertility clinics.) Youth offers fresh perspectives and are more likely to offer assistance in an urgent situation than one that appears ideal. And when needed, kids may discover their own power tools.

TWENTY-FOUR CARROTS

I'm forever surprised by the lure of the simple cookie. The actions of toddlers can be directed almost anywhere with these treats. Crackers and certain cereals work well though only if the sugary stuff is delayed. Such bribes ease the lives of parents and are useful— but short-lived. The cookie's value wanes when the location of the cookie jar is discovered. Knowing the source forever changes all matters. Sweets cease to entice kids to do adult bidding when they discover how to fill their own sweet tooth with those countless comfort foods. Those tangible items, rewards like food or money move us. And I call them *carats*. (Sometimes spelled with a "k.") I can reward myself with such carats, or someone who has a stake in my actions might offer me one. But carats are distinct from those mysterious incentives, I label *carrots*. Carrots, grown personally, are intangible and trickier to detect. What really moves us to action?

Food and treats of all sorts motivate pets, who reap the rewards of the multibillion dollar pet industry in America today. Suggestions such as "walk?" and "car-ride?", short words that pets come to understand, get them to follow owners' wishes. Rousing domesticated animals is simple. Their survival needs are plain. Though like most things, there are puzzling exceptions. Ordinary carats such as food didn't work for Seabiscuit. His biographer tells us that the he was once passive and difficult to rouse. But he became one of the few horses famous enough to have an actual biography—that became a best seller that morphed into a famous movie in the U.S. Seemingly smart, Seabiscuit showed little interest in his world and slept all day at a young age when horses are filled with energy. A gloomy sign for a horse. In the end, he became a historic *race*horse, mysteriously motivated by a trainer who installed two stall-mates. Who would have guessed that that the horse needed friends.

Questions about motivation were forever posed to me by the parents. Easily identified, smart kids too can be lost at the gate as they *turn off* to formal schooling and dropout. Intelligence is far from a single, motivational marker. Sometimes sports and curriculum extras entice a few reluctant strays but not always. Parents and the school offer carats— in the form of money and grades. But eventually kids have to *grow* their own carrots—and the job can't be farmed *for* them. I had this illustrated in a remarkable family that once skipped across my life. Educators are lucky to have even *one* shining case in the annals of their careers so I was spellbound in the years it took these five siblings to pass through high school. All were liked by their peers, played musical instruments as well as sports, and with outstanding grades, all won full scholarships to Ivy League colleges. All ranked either first or second in graduating classes of over two hundred. To say the least, their high school years were balanced. I've often guessed about the genes that led them to this pinnacle: superior intelligence? physical attractiveness? nurturing? attentive parents with strong values? But I had seen all these variables in the past, yielding nothing close to the motivation I saw in these five siblings.

Maybe it was a combination of all these factors. Maybe everything came together in the right environment for those five, just as some planets align in a unique fashion once in a century. But the fact that not one rebel emerged, not one was *un*motivated turning off to the scholastic or social demands of a public school, finally piqued my interest. Something positive was happening in that home. And I began to ask questions.

The parents reported that they never offered rewards for good grades. Knowing that only one parent had a monetary income, I saw that they couldn't have afforded rewards for five offsprings— through twelve years of public schooling. As their kids began to make decisions, I learned that the parents never tried to rescue them—saving them from the consequences of poor choices. If one of the kids signed up for a class they later disliked because of teacher or subject matter, parents denied permission to drop it. Since the original decision to take the course had been the students', parents refused to get involved after the fact. Kids learned early that *their* decisions were significant. No one tried to save these five from poor decisions—with that arrogant *I told you so* scenario. No helicopter parents here.

I learned things from these parents that had never graced the pages of parenting books. At least not in the many that I'd read. Older siblings tutored younger ones in a room in their home devoted solely to schoolwork. References of all sorts adorned this sacred space where only study took place. Education ranked high in this home—to a palpable point. Because older siblings tutored younger ones, poor grades disappointed siblings not just parents, as usually happens. This family didn't need a hero. They were all heroes.

To hear of the carrots grown by the kids themselves, I turned to Patrick, the second son. "We kids have created the family name in this town. Such renown wouldn't exist without us" he calmly informed me as I sat in my seat. Stunned. Helping to shape the family surname in the community had motivated Patrick. Putting two and two together as he spoke, I remembered the socio-economic side of the family, knowing that their home came slightly short of a shack in the town. Rather than shamed by this fact, Patrick felt pride in his contribution to the family name—pride that he and his siblings had developed a family reputation through their excellence in school. The dazzling family name in the community hinged on the efforts of each child—not on the family income or a snazzy house and car. Though I knew them, I never interviewed the other siblings; their school records seemed in harmony with Patrick's account. I learned two big things from this family. Kids learn to trust their decisions through facing consequences and are moved to do their best when making a contribution.

Emotional needs enter the scenario and snarl this riddle of motivation. That spur switch stumps science because the answer doesn't lie in measurable intelligence or money. There's no direct ratio between high motivation and tangible things. The prospects of poor health or even death fail to motivate cigarette smokers to quit. Lighting the cigarette is a little like the reward of that long ago sweet. Though now lacking the worrisome calories of those old carats, the cigarette holds more deadly concerns. For me, the threat of lung cancer is a strong incentive not to smoke—a good reason to end the smelly business. But my reasoning, to save one life or even more since the effects of secondhand smoke are known, falls short for some smokers. Those who find no reason to quit likely feel they can't impact their own health and adopt the passive mantra: *We all die of something.*

Dire situations don't always depress people into passive lives either. *Bad* situations sometimes motivate—in a good way. Children of alcoholics (COA in its official clipped version) are often thrown into the role of caretaker in a family. As no one else is running the show. Managing to become responsible early in life, COAs are often labeled *high achievers* in both school and life. Though argued that these kids pay a high price for their success, their zeal goes without doubt. While at the other end of the spectrum lie children who offered every opportunity by caring parents struggle to find the passion necessary for action.

Passion. It takes passion to cultivate those self-grown carrots.

Those passionless kids who forever claim *I'm bored* can't see how *their* actions make a difference. The COA who steps in to accept adult responsibilities detects from the start that their contribution is needed. As a dividend, COAs learn their strengths firsthand. Also starting from scratch, immigrants to America are often highly motivated and leave amazing legacies.

Adolph Hitler's passion resulted in the design of the gas-saving VW Bug. As well as the horrific deaths of hundreds of thousands of innocent people. As with this tyrant of our time, motivation can travel in either or both directions. What stirred John D Rockefeller to make all of that money? According to his biographer, Rockefeller was motivated to clean up his surname, the name his derelict father had blackened. Unlike the five in my story who enhanced the family surname, Rockefeller began with a higher mountain to climb. But his fortune resulted in historic generosity that forever sanctified the name Rockefeller.

Walter Isaacson's biography of personal computer giant Steve Jobs' implies that Jobs was moved to show his birth parents what they'd lost in giving him up at birth. Leonardo DaVinci, whose feats need no comment from me, was the bastard son of a wealthy Italian who never legalized the boy. Both men likely hoped to impress on natural parents their losses. But neither spent a depressed life. Both Jobs and DaVinci were passionate men who left legacies that will enhance the world—for a very long time. Carrots come from the inside and are about contribution. We might be moved by the tangible carats but grow more potent carrots ourselves.

FOOTINGS

I knew little of the Great Wall of China through most of my life. Short of location. But I got curious at the beginning of the twenty-first century when the news media reported the uncovering of hundreds of *additional* miles of the already two-thousand-mile barrier— begun 200 BC. I performed a bit of research and found that at a height of twenty-five feet, the structure is twice the height of the infamous Berlin Wall. With a length of over 3000 miles, the Great Wall could stretch across the United States. And there may be more yet to be uncovered. I don't know if such an edifice ever proved effective protection for China, but it's certainly a notable construction. As the only artificial object visible from the moon, the barrier conquers space. No other man-made object on Earth can be identified from such a distance: 238,857 miles. A distance that equals ten trips around the world. The Great Wall raises for me the age-old question of perpetuity. What endures the test of time? What lasts?

Forever seems a bit fanciful for debate given that human bodies self-destruct in a maximum of 135 years. (A few have lasted this long so biologists claim this figure as the human life span.) Since the earth is roughly five billion years old, 135 years is a drop in the bucket. Still, while they endure bodies house huge brains that have given us the foresight to create such things as time capsules— with an eye on forever. Time capsules transport a mixture of artifacts that inform new generations about a past they'll never know. Future generations will never interact with most of these objects, except perhaps as antiques. What was life like before texting? Before cell phones? Before computers? Before cars? Mirrors? Glass? Fire? Before human speech? The capsule items will answer a few questions for future inhabitants of the planet. But what about the items that can't be stuffed into containers? How are the intangibles passed on?

My mother taught me two lessons about life's intangibles. For her, they were nonnegotiables action, closed to discussion. One never missed Sunday Mass and the family, evening meal was at 5:30 PM. Seemingly simple things that she never put into words. My mother laid down no dictums. I got her message through a thing called ritual. Dinner was always on the table at exactly 5:30. If I arrived at 5:35, barring paralysis I was declared *late*, as though the tardy bell had rung. Sunday morning was church unless I was a bedridden kind of sick. I quickly learned that there was no leeway in either case. And even excuses that seemed reasonable to me were useless.

Frustrated but with no choice, I finally settled into these daily and weekly ceremonies of my youth. And accepted that these two events were preset, not open to either discussion or bargains with my mother. Eventually I saw that both also required much of her. *Her* self-discipline put the food on the table at the precise time. And she *practiced what she preached* by never missing Mass herself. I felt secure knowing that a nice dinner would be on the table and learned things at the church service that would stay with me, even after my spiritual life changed. That rigid dinner hour and the required church service didn't follow me into adulthood. But the wordless power of self-discipline and ritual did.

Since language sets me apart from other mammals, it's hard to admit but some things are bigger than words. And ritual is usually wordless, carrying those intangibles through the generations— hand-delivering them in actions, not words. Pointing up the old cliché, *actions speak louder than words*. At the Olympics, the ritual of passing the torch is acted out by a quiet runner. The centuries old justice system in the courts is denoted by the long black robes. No one speaks of updating the garb of either the justices or religious priests in twenty-first America. The ancient attire strips the wearers of the ordinary and sets them apart. But neither the robes nor the torch would mean much in a time capsules—nor would an exact dinner hour or church attendance. The story's bigger than material things.

The ritual of the modern Olympics tells me that Ancient Greece valued the potential of the human body. These three thousand years old athletic contests, though modernized, are so popular today that countries around the world compete to host them. Martial Arts, also a thousand year old practice, originated in the far east of China, Japan and Korea. Martial means military or warlike, but Martial Arts are all about unarmed combat. Encouraging confidence in participants, Martial Arts removes the need to declare winners and losers in physical conflicts. Using words to declare that the human body is a work of art is meaningless compared to the rituals that accompany the Olympics and the Martial Arts.

Tradition, another word for ritual, opens the popular musical Fiddler on the Roof. The main character sings that all humans live as fiddlers, forever shaky standing on rooftops—in our feeble attempt to be seen and heard. "It's tradition" that keeps us balanced on that shaky rooftop the singer bellows. The demise of one of the practices at the end of the 19th century comes about but other rituals endure and transcend even the deepest emotions of the characters of the play. The play concludes that some traditions aren't worth the transportation fee to the future and are allowed to die.

One ritual that has died in the culture is gossip. Though only its original form; we humans still gossip about one another. Derived from the word *godsipp*, gossip originated from midwives who once taught that the pain of childbirth could be lessened through local chitchat. The midwives distracted the laboring women with village gossip. Though this ritual was worded, the godsipp seemed effective in those days before drugs. And was obviously safer.

Most ritual demands repetition stressing the physical over verbal actions. Some rituals put music to use in the form of cyclic chanting and drumming. Rites of Passage rituals differ by religion and culture but have the same purpose—to ease life transitions. Such customs as baptism, first communion, bar mitzvah and marriage make the change easier, and last rites and funerals are designed to relieve the pain of loss. Cultural customs, another name for ritual, require participants to suspend segments of their days—regardless of circumstances. The English stop and have their tea just as the Mexicans take their afternoon siestas. Though they vary in content by culture, it's clear that the message is bigger than either tea or naps. The *intrusion* of these practices into daily lives forces—a bigger view of life.

Meditation is a form of ritual that encourages participants to leave the visible world— that world of both joy and heartbreak—and experience the inner world. The meditative state requires solemn attention to an inner world that can be so intense that changes in the brain have been recorded during these periods. Meditation's lasting effects, like the process itself, remain wordless. In the rather risky ritual of fire-walking, neurological changes are obviously required. Otherwise the walkers would quickly be doomed to cremation.

Religion is steeped in ritual. Christian churches dramatize the birth and resurrection of Jesus during the annual celebration of these holidays. When Muslims repeat their daily prayers several times a day, they turn towards Mecca, their most sacred city. Some religious rituals are private and held in homes, as the twenty-four hour Jewish Sabbath that stresses reflection and family. Through wordless drama and repetition, the practices pass on messages about life's nonnegotiables.

Ritual persists because we need to know about those preset things. Those items closed to debate. Why else are Americans so fascinated with the ancient ceremony that surrounds the British royalty? Which is quite costly for English citizens. Hints of ritual can be seen among American high school kids. Some kids practice an ancient rite with body tattoos and piercings. Labeled neo-Nazis, some kids dress in long trench coats to capture the era of the thirties and forties in Germany and are known among their peers as the "trench coat mafia." I doubt that this neo-Nazis group of seventeen year olds knows the full history of fascism and the horror of genocide, but ritual is a practice that mesmerizes them. Satanic worship, enveloped in ritual, reveals itself in youthful music. Shaved heads, pierced bodies, weirdly dyed hair, and black clothing, known as "Goth" appear in today's schools. The origins rest in a distant past, often unknown to young followers who seem entranced by the power of ritual. Though they seldom articulate the sentiment, kids look for their link to a past far beyond their parents. Beyond the history books. They're searching for a foothold. A foundation.

We humans, not time capsules, transmit the intangibles through our rituals.

Though the Great Wall is no longer a protective barrier for China, it stands as a metaphor for me. A reminder that those nonnegotiables are big, making me part of a much bigger story. And the image assures me that I'm not alone. That I have a foothold in the past as well as the present. Like standing on the summit of a mountain, or on the Great Wall itself, I have a panorama —a fuller picture of life that brings me to my knees. I'm grateful, and it matters not to What or Whom.

OVER THE RAINBOW

I listened to a talk show recently that offered solutions to those little bothers around the home. In the name of convenience, the commentator suggested household products to use on such things as that steamed, bathroom mirror. The broadcast guidance advised spreading a substance over the mirror before showering. Which later had to be removed. The dual action took longer and was more costly than the proven alternative—open the bathroom door after a hot shower. Forever analyzing even trivial troubles reveal more *woes* to capture our attention. *Woes me*, as the saying goes. Depression and mental illness are publicized in the media, while simple statistics on the joyful amongst us is scarce. Under heaps of information on illnesses of all sorts, the roots of happiness remain elusive: either fly over the rainbow to find it or get a good night's sleep, eat well and exercise. What is happiness? Can it be defined?

I'm happy when not sad. There it is, a quickie in the twenty-first century where speed is the password to nearly everything. More formally stated: *Happiness is the absence of gloom.* After cleaning out the despair, I settle for what's left? This puts happiness in the default category, where no choices are made. A happy face seems a bit shallow in light of the words used to express happiness in the English language: joy, delight, satisfaction, pleasure, bliss, euphoria, exhilaration, elation, rapture, glee, delight, comfort, security, success, jubilance, contentment. On and on. Likewise, the Eskimos have lots of words for— what else, snow. With so many words that express it, happiness is pretty important.

Another try. *Happiness is a desired state of being.* But this one too is flawed. Though it's several notches above the previous definition, the state can't be endless. Monotony sets in and thus a paradox appears. That *desired state* must end in order to classify as happiness. Happiness evaporates when the experience is infinite—and could be the root of the *quit while you're ahead* counsel. Honeymoons are defined periods, with a beginning and an ending. Otherwise they wouldn't carry connotations of bliss.

The joy of one particular vacation in my life remained with me for months. I hold wonderful memories of that week. But had I remained there—expecting a permanent state of bliss— my memories would be different, most likely far less exciting. The week granted intangible souvenirs that lightened *me* and thus my suitcase. My suitcase was easier to carry when I left to return home. I'd become stronger but not in muscle power. From the start, I knew the time was exactly seven days. An unplanned sojourn, one of those last minute decisions, the week was helped along by my lack of expectation. I had no recommendations, no reason to expect anything extraordinary. No travel agent had promised me the *time of my life.*

It was the summer of 1981. The national, front-page news that August carried opposing messages: romance and tragedy of physical love hung in the air. There was Prince Charles and Diana, a royal love affair that charmed the world. Charles, the crown prince of England, had searched for years, so royalty watchers assumed, to find the "right" woman. And he had at last found her—working around the corner from Buckingham Palace, at a London kindergarten. Contrary to England's mesmerizing love story was the sudden appearance of a strange illness among the gay, male community on the West Coast of the United States. Men were dying, but the medical world couldn't identify the cause so the illness was nameless, making it even scarier— and fodder for the still large, anti-gay society in America. The divergent but human stories flooded the news that August and created an atmosphere of haziness. Life felt less certain as eternal love came face to face with premature death.

Such a mood gave me a second reason for a personal retreat. Working in public schools, I was soon to return to a hectic schedule. As *last minute* implies, I had no time to shop for what I *needed*. The week was a casual conference on the coast of Maine so a bathing suit was in order— and likely my only need beyond the basics. Had I listened and read the ads, those colorful reminders that seem to forever forecast all wants, wishes and needs, even ones that are yet known, I would likely have bought some special clothes, a new camera, a kayak. On and on. Ads imply that material items deliver delight: smoking a particular cigarette: drinking a special brand of vodka promise to carry joy— buying the *right* things might even land a soul mate at the front door.

Forever advising how to *pursue* happiness, advertisements sometimes put me off course. I was in pursuit of one thing that summer. A low-priced getaway where I could relax before returning to a long, school year. In addition to my lack of time, I couldn't afford much from a teacher's salary. And anyway, I had given up pursuits of any kind. As a kid, I had learned that it was only when I discarded the net that a colorful butterfly often landed on my shoulder. Even when I'd occasionally catch that butterfly, it proved the wrong kind. In the *happily ever after* fairy tale, the handsome prince, a metaphor like the butterfly, is disguised as a frog. And his attributes are valued only by the vigilant— those who lack a draft of the desire: those who leave their options open in regard that prince's appearance. While the majority of us earthlings, carry a mental blueprint as to what will make us happy, carefully recorded in our psyches.

Had I exceeded my budget and bought those advertised tangibles to *make me happy* that unplanned week in '81, I could then have returned to the same *pot of gold* (some program, store or website) for second helpings anytime, expecting the same joyful outcome. But life doesn't work that way. At least not for me. Water is only a joy when it's scarce. Each Christmas season, one kid's toy is the rage, and a shortage increases with the approach of the holiday— so the toy becomes more valuable. Though the coup of the plaything delivers a momentary pleasure to both the buyer and child, the same toy will never have another such day in the sun. As tangibles become plentiful, their worth as a source of joy diminishes. (Merchants well know this painful truth.)

In addition to my lack of goods, my experience that summer week was in a rustic location that lacked convenience. And caused moments of stress. But the atmosphere of uncertainty throughout the Western world in '81 gave me a sense of freedom—nothing was set in stone. New rules seemed possible, and I became deeply absorbed in the program, and got through the stress of participant rather than spectator at the conference. I focused on the people who surrounded me and got to know all twelve of them on an amazingly deep level—all became memorable. That week, I didn't grapple with thoughts of my appearance. Or theirs. Or status. Or theirs. Or issues like a foggy bathroom mirror. Or even asking myself if I was happy. All of which gave happiness a better shot at me. That week I learned that happiness wasn't elusive at all. Though joyless on the surface, the tough events made demands on me. But carried dividends.

Research supports my meager meanderings. Dr Janet DiPetietro, a developmental psychologist at John Hopkins, writes: "Most people do their best when under moderate stress." Evolutionary biologists make the point even stronger, writing that two and a half million years ago the *stress* of constant weather change in east Africa caused major increases in human brain development. Stress has served humans.

In her book *Ice Bound*, a forty-six year old doctor, Jerri Nielsen, recounts isolated months spent at the South Pole. She had purposely joined the expedition searching for a daring job; in this unusual environment she would give the researchers access to medical care. With temperatures averaging fifty degrees below zero, in close quarters with forty other people and eventually ill herself, she describes the year as the *happiest* of her life. Dr Nielsen concludes that the experience demanded that she be creative and finally led to self-discovery. Her happiness was a *side effect* of the original goal. With her own illness and other responsibilities in the forsaken land, Dr Nielsen focused on her power. Not power over others but simply the enormity of her own abilities.

I would call Dr Nielsen's experience "challenging." Maybe a rare learning experience— but hardly earning my label of happy. Likewise, most likely many would not find my extraordinary week extraordinary at all. Maybe not *un*happy but hyperbole on my part— I doubt it will elicit envy from readers. Happiness is a personal call. One that could eliminate envy from our lexicon. That painful emotion of envy slips away when those judgment calls on others' happiness halts. Appraisal from the outside is always sketchy—at best. Which is why the courts don't allow testimony that's secondhand. "Hearsay" judges declare.

Carrying a blueprint of what makes me happy omits options. And hope often hinders happiness. A definition is at hand. *Happiness is a finite state, an offshoot turning up when sights are focused elsewhere. An intense experience, happiness can neither be bought or sought. Finally it can only be measured by the owner and never prescribed.*

All of this paradox may account for the fact that data on happiness is hard to come by. But its study could be useful in schools today. Common thought is that kids enjoy themselves much too much these days. That more self-discipline, less instant gratification, is in order. Still those *bored* (their adjective not mine) teenagers of the twenty-first century appear in search of something. And maybe joy, stripped of material goods, deserves a place alongside the other subjects offered at the table of mandated schooling. Considering that a popular, recreational drug among the young today is dubbed Ecstasy, and a previous one was known as Angel Dust, a worthwhile enterprise would be to add the study of happiness to the school curriculum. Good information on the subject can empower kids— offering them a fair shot at this emotion known as happiness.

SELECTED BIBLIOGRAPHY

Allport, Gordon. <u>Becoming</u>, New Haven: Yale University Press, 1955

Amaya, Mario. <u>Tiffany Glass,</u> Toronto: Ryerson Press, 1967

Ansbacher, Heinz & Rowena. <u>The Individual Psychology of Alfred Adler:</u> N Y: Basic Books, 1956

Bannister, Roger. <u>Four Minute Mile,</u> England: Lyons and Burford, 1955

Biehler, R. <u>Child Development,</u> Boston, Mass: Houghton-Mifflin, 1981

Bly, Robert. <u>The Sibling Society,</u> N Y, N Y: Vintage Books, 1996

Bohn, David. & Peat, David. <u>Science, Order, and Creativity,</u> N Y, N Y: Bantam Books, 1987

Borysenko, Joan. <u>Minding the Body, Mending the Mind,</u> Boston, Mass: Addison-Wesley, 1987

Brunner, Jerome. <u>Toward a Theory of Instruction</u>, Cambridge, Mass: Belkap Press, 1966

Casteneda, Carlos. <u>Journey to Ixtlan,</u> N Y: Simon and Shuster,1972

Chernow, Ron. <u>Titan: The life of John D Rockefeller,</u> NY, NY: Random House, 1998

Coles, Robert. <u>The Spiritual Lives of Children,</u> Boston, Mass: Houghton-Mifflin, 1990

Csikszentmihalyi, Mihaly. <u>Flow</u>, N Y, N Y: Harper and Row, 1990

Damon, William. <u>Greater Expectations,</u> N Y, N Y: The Free Press, 1995

Dossey, Larry. <u>Healing Words,</u> N Y, N Y: Harper-Collins, 1993

Fortey, Richard. <u>Horseshoe Crabs and Velvet Worms: What Time has left Behind,</u> NY, NY:Knopf,2012

Fowles, John. <u>The Tree,</u> N Y, N Y: Little Brown, 1980

_____ <u>The Aristos,</u> Boston, Mass:Little Brown, 1970

Gibsen, K, Lathrop, D, Mare, E. <u>Carl Jung & Soul Psychology</u>, N Y: Harrington Park Press, 1991

Gladwell, Malcom <u>The Tipping Point,</u> Boston, Mass: Little Brown, 2002

Hillenbrand, Laura<u>. Seabiscuit,</u> New York: Random House, 2003

Huxley, Aldous. <u>Brave New World</u>, New York: Harper & Row, 1932

Ishiguro, Kazuo <u>Never Let Me Go,</u> Knopf Doubleday Publishing Group, 2006

Keen, Sam. <u>Learning to Fly</u>, California: Harper, 1992

_____ <u>To Love and Be Loved,</u> New York, NY: Bantam Books, 1997

_____ <u>Fire In the Belly,</u> New York, NY:Bantam Books, 1991

Kopp, Sheldon. <u>If You Meet the Buddha Along the Way, Kill Him</u>, California: Science & Behavior Books, 1972

Langer, Ellen. <u>Mindfulness</u>, Boston, Mass: Addison-Wesley, 1989

Lilly, John. <u>The Center of the Cyclone,</u> New York, NY, Julian Press, 1972

Lvy, William <u>Hand Making America</u>

May, Rolo. <u>Man's Search for Himself,</u> N Y: W W Norton: 1952

Moore, Thomas. <u>Care of the Soul,</u> NY, NY: Harper Collins, 1992

Myss, Carolyn. <u>Anatomy of the Spirit,</u> N Y, N Y: Random House, 1996

_____ <u>Sacred Contracts,</u> N Y: Harmony House, 2001

_____ <u>Why People Don't Heal and How They Can,</u> N Y: Three Rivers Press, 1997

_____ <u>Defy Gravity,</u> Australia, Hay House, 2009

Nielsen, Jerri. <u>Ice Bound</u>, N Y: Hyperion, 2001

Piaget, Jean, <u>The Child's Conception of the World</u>, N Y: Humanities, 1951

Pearce, Joseph Chilton. <u>The Crack in The Cosmic Egg</u>, NY, NY: Simon and Shuster, 1971

_____ <u>The Magical Child,</u> NY, NY: EP Dutton, 1977

_____ <u>The Death of Religion and the Rebirth of Spirit</u>, Rochester, Vt: Inner Traditions, 2007

_____ <u>The Biology of Transcendence,</u> Rochester, Vt: Inner Traditions, 2002

Prather, Hugh. <u>Circle of Thought,</u> Texas: Amethsts & Aura, 1987

Rogers, Carl. <u>On Personal Power,</u> N Y: Delacorte Press, 1977

Sardello, Robert. <u>Love and the World,</u> Great Barrington, MA: Lindisfarne Books, 2001

Satir, Virginia. <u>Peoplemaking,</u> Calif: Science and Behavior Books, 1972

Slater, Phillip. <u>The Pursuit of Loneliness</u>, Boston: Beacon Press, 1970

Smith, Huston. <u>Why Religion Matters,</u> N Y: Harper Collins, 2001

Steyer, James. <u>Talking Back to Facebook</u>, NY, NY Scribner 2007

Straus, Peter. <u>World History,</u> N Y, NY: Houghton Mifflin, 2001

Talbot, Michael, <u>Mysticism and The New Physics</u>, N Y, N Y: Bantam Books, 1981

Taylor, Jeremy. <u>Where People Fly and Water Runs Up Hill</u>, N Y, N Y: Warner Books, 1992

Terkle, Sheryl. <u>Together Alone</u>, NY, NY: Basic Books, 2011

Thomas, Lewis, <u>Lives of a Cell</u>, N Y, NY: Viking Press,1974

Tofler, Alvin, <u>Future Shock,</u> N Y, Random House, 1970

Tolle, Eckhart, <u>The Power of Now</u>, Canada, Namaste, 2004

Watson, Lyall, <u>Lifetide</u>, N Y, N Y: Simon & Shuster, 1979

_____ <u>Beyond Supernature,</u> N Y: Bantam Books, 1988

Watts, Alan, <u>The Spirit of Zen,</u> N Y, N Y: Macmillian,1960

Weil, Andrew. <u>Health and Healing</u>, Boston: Houghton-Mifflin, 1998

Williamson, Marianne <u>A Woman's Worth</u>, NY, NY: Random House, 1993

Zukav, Gary, <u>The Dancing Wu Li Masters</u>, N Y: Murrow, 1979

_____ <u>Seat of the Soul,</u> Fireside, N Y, N Y: 1990

Newsweek: vol cl104, no3, *Searching for the God Within* pg 59

Newsweek: vol cl111, no8 *Stress Could Save Your Life* pg 46

Newsweek: volclvl, no3, *The Creativity Crisis pg 45*

Newsweek: volclvll, no2/3 *Can You Build a Better Brain? pg 42*

Physics World: vol23, no 6 *Symbols of Power* pg 23

Time: vol167, no 16, *Dropout Nation* pg 30

Time: vol163, no 8, *The Secret Killer* pg 38

Time: vol181, no12, *How to Cure Cancer pg30*